SIMLA
THEN & NOW

Summer Capital of the Raj

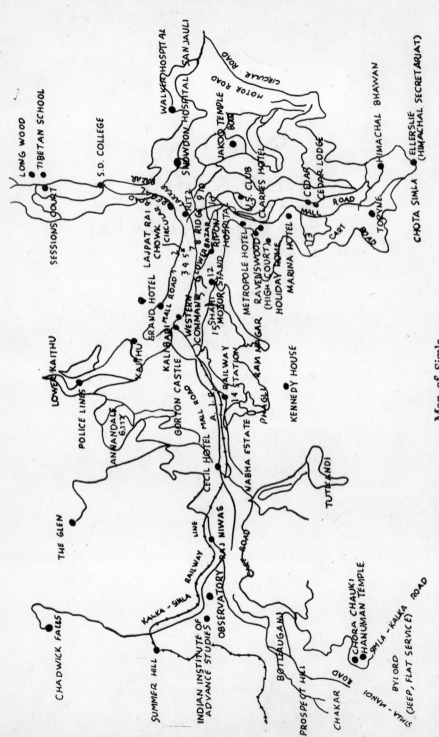

Map of Simla

SIMLA
THEN & NOW

Summer Capital of the Raj

Vipin Pubby

INDUS PUBLISHING COMPANY, NEW DELHI

© 1988 Indus Publishing Company, New Delhi

First published in 1988 by
Indus Publishing Company
FS-5, Tagore Garden, New Delhi 110027

ISBN 81–85182–11–6

Published by M.L. Gidwani, Indus Publishing Company
FS-5, Tagore Garden, New Delhi 110027, and printed at
Gidson Printing Works, FS-5, Tagore Garden, New Delhi

Acknowledgements

It would not have been possible to complete the book without the whole-hearted, sincere and invaluable help rendered by Mian Goverdhan Singh, Chief Librarian, Himachal Pradesh State Secretariat Library, Simla. His vast knowledge and personal interest in the subject has been of tremendous help. It is also difficult to express gratitude for the great pains taken by Prof. S.R. Mehrotra of the History Department of the Himachal Pradesh University, Simla. His encouragement and suggestions have made it possible to complete this work. My friend and colleague Swadesh Talwar has kindly let me use some of his beautiful pictures. Thanks are also due to numerous friends and well-wishers who constantly encouraged me in this venture. And finally my thanks are due to my wife Shashi who lent the moral support and created a congenial atmosphere for the efforts put in to complete the book.

VIPIN PUBBY

To
All lovers of Simla

Preface

Simla occupies a unique place in the history of the Indian sub-continent. Emerging as a nostalgic reminder of their country for the British officers posted in the region, the town went on to occupy the centre-stage during the hey-day of the Raj. The decisions taken at the summer capital of the Indian Empire directly affected millions of people in the sub-continent and directed the course of history. The town became a symbol of the British power. On the one hand it was criticised for the fun and frivolity which was associated with the British social life, on the other it came in for severe criticism for being detached from the people and reality—"government working from the 500th floor" as Gandhiji put it—and finally, the rise of nationalist movement saw a decline in its influence and importance. Simla was the site of several historic and momentous decisions taken during the freedom struggle which ultimately led to the partition of the country and its independence.

Despite the historic importance of the town, one does not find any comprehensive account of the events which occurred during the last two centuries. Western travellers and residents have left detailed accounts of the life at Simla till the beginning of the 20th century. However, no such account by any Indian is available. There is also an absence of any comprehensive work on the pre-independence years in Simla. Not only the visitors and tourists to the town remain unaware of the historic importance of the town, many new and younger residents of the former summer capital of India are also ignorant of its history. It is hoped that this book would fulfil a long-felt need in providing a chronological account of events that took place in Simla. Though officially the name of the town is now spelt as 'Shimla', old spellings have been retained just for the sake of uniformity.

VIPIN PUBBY

Contents

List of Illustrations

AN OLD SONG*

So long as 'neath the Kalka hills
    The tonga-horn shall ring,
So long as down the Solon dip
    The hard-held ponies swing.

So long as Tara Devi sees
    The lights of Simla town,
So long as Pleasure calls us up,
    Or Duty drives us down,
        If you love me as I love you
        What pair so happy as we two?

So long as Aces take the King,
    Or backers take the bet,
So long as debt leads men to wed,
    Or marriage leads to debt,
So long as little luncheons, Love,
    And scandal hold their vogue,
While there is sport at Annandale
    Or whisky at Jutogh,
        If you love me as I love you
        What knife can cut our love in two?

So long as down the rocking floor
    The raving polka spins,
So long as Kitchen Lancers spur
    The maddened violins,
So long as through the whirling smoke
    We hear the oft-told tale—
"Twelve hundred in the Lotteries,"
    And Whats her name for sale,
        If you love me as I love you
        We'll play the game and win it too.

*Rudyard Kipling's Verse: *Definitive Edition* (1977), pp. 58-60.

So long as Lust and Lucre tempt
    Straight riders from the course,
So long as with each drink we pour
    Black beverage of Remorse,
So long as those unloaded guns
    We keep beside the bed,
Blow off, by obvious accident,
    The lucky owner's head,
        If you love me as I love you
        What can Life kill or Death undo?

So long as Death 'twixt dance and dance
    Chills best and bravest blood,
And drops the reckless rider down
    The rotten, rain-soaked *khud*,
So long as rumours from the North
    Make loving wives afraid,
So long as Burma takes the boy
    Or typhoid kills the maid,
        If you love me as I love you
        What knife can cut our love in two?

By all that lights our daily life
    Or works our life-long woe,
From Boileauganj to Simla Town
    And those grim glades below,
Where, heedless of the flying hoof
    And clamour overhead
Sleep, with the grey langur for guard,
    Our very scornful Dead,
        If you love me as I love you
        All Earth is servant to us two!

By Docket, Billetdoux, and File,
    By Mountain, Cliff, and Fir,
By Fan and Sword and Office-box,
    By Corset, Plume, and Spur
By Riot, Revel, Waltz, and War,
    By Women, Work, and Bills,
By all the life that fizzes in
    The everlasting Hills,
        If you love me as I love you
        What pair so happy as we two?

A LETTER BY LORD DUFFERIN*

"We have now come up to Simla, an absurd place situated on the narrow saddle of one of a hundred mountainous ridges that rise around us in labyrinthine complexity like the waves of a confused and troubled sea, composing the lower ranges of the Himalayas, whose silver peaks stand up against the horizon some fifty miles away. We ourselves are at a height of seven thousand feet above the sea. The air is delicious, most healthy and bracing, but anything more funny than the appearance of the town you cannot imagine. It consists of innumerable little miniature Swiss cottages which are perched like toy houses in every nook and corner and cranny where they can get a foothold on the ridge of a Himalayan spur. It looks like a place of which a child might dream after seeing a pantomime. If you look up from your garden-seat you see the gables of a cottage tumbling down on the top of you. If you lean over your terrace wall you look down your neighbour's chimney-pots. That the capital of the Indian empire should be thus hanging on by its eyelids to the side of a hill is too absurd. But there are the most charming walks—shady paths cut into the side of the mountain up and down hill in every direction, and wherever you go splendid rhododendrons thirty feet high covered with blossoms, while whole tribes of monkeys spring from branch to branch of the thick growing trees."

*An extract from a letter by Lord Dufferin to Lady Dartrey, 15 May 1885; Dufferin Papers.

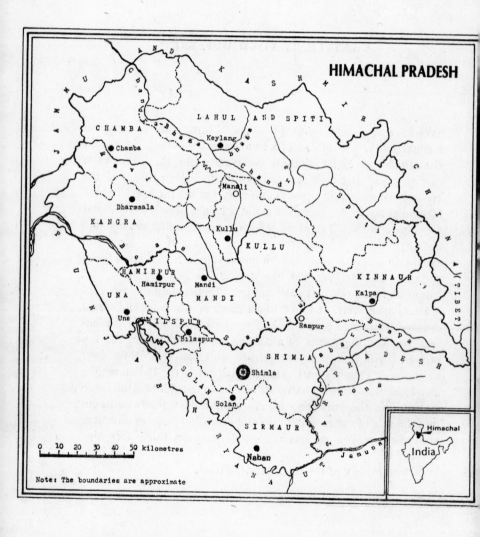

1
The Early Times
1805–1860

Barely two centuries ago, the area occupied by the modern-day Simla was a dense forest. Only the Jakhu temple, which has stood the test of time, and a few scattered houses comprised the signs of civilisation. For a lack of contemporary history, opinion is divided even over the origin of its name. While some assert that the name is derived from a solitary house called 'Shamlaey', others believe that the name is a derivative from the name of a village called 'Shimlah' or 'Shumlah'. A few others believe that a temple of goddess 'Shamli' gave birth to the modern name but others assert that its original name was 'Shyamalaya'. Indeed very little is known about its early history. The earliest available records reveal that the area formed a part of the Keonthal State at the turn of the 18th century.

The "British connection" with the area had its roots in the battle of Kangra between the Sikhs and the Gurkhas during 1804. The Sikh army had inflicted a crushing defeat on the Gurkhas which had forced them to retreat and take shelter in the hills. It was during that time that the Gurkhas had constructed several forts after over-running small chieftains. If one were to totally rely on the accounts left by the British, the Gurkhas spread a reign of terror "until at length the people in their wretchedness appealed to the British for help." An official record, pertaining to the "excesses" committed by the Gurkhas, quotes one Udhat Singh Keonar as complaining that they "ate so many goats that the price of these useful animals rose to Rs. 30 per head."

Therefore the British, the record states, resolved to "expel" the Gurkhas from the hill territories. Some historians assert that it was merely an excuse to annexe the strategic hill areas. In this context it would be interesting to study a letter written on January 6, 1850 by the then Superintendent of Hill States, W. Edwards to P. Melvill, Secretary of the Board of Administration, Lahore, which has been cited by the first regular settlement report of Simla district to assert that the British had "no intention" to annexe the area.

It states that the "rugged nature of the country and the small British force—a single division under Major General Sir David Ochterlony—which could be spared made it imperative to secure the aid of the hillmen in the expulsion of the common enemy. With this object and as, moreover, it was not our policy to annexe territory in the hills, proclamations were issued inviting the cooperation of the chiefs and people, and declaring our intention of re-instating the chiefs who had been expelled by the Gurkhas and having restored matters to the condition before the Gurkha invasion, of withdrawing altogether from that part of the country." The same account claims that a majority of hill chiefs responded to the call and joined the British army in the fight against the Gurkhas. Though Gurkhas are known to be excellent warriors, they lost one fort after the other solely due to the superior fire power of the British. The rivals were engaged in the toughest battle at the 3750-feet high Ramgarh fort at Nalagarh. A desperate battle took place near the fort at Malaon. The Gurkhas fought valiantly and, as a last resort, even charged to the muzzles of the guns but superior gun power led to their defeat. Their leader Bhagta Thapa was slain and the British captured the fort.

The British, with their tradition of honouring the valiant, raised the first Gurkha Rifles in the Malaon fort. It was the first Gurkha batallion to enter the British army and till today retains the name of Malaon Rifles in commemoration of the fort. A brass plaque was also placed near a banyan tree just outside the fort but it disappeared several years ago. The Gurkha resistance, therefore, ended with the battle at Malaon on May 15, 1815. Sir David Ochterlony issued an official proclamation a few days after the battle that all chieftains who had joined the British in expelling the Gurkhas would have their land restored "and should enjoy the benefits of our protection, as well as their previous rights and privileges." However, it soon became apparent, states the letter, that "it would be impracticable for us to abandon the country on expulsion of the enemy as the government had desired, on the contrary, in order to maintain our guarantee of protection not only against the foreign enemy, but to retain in their ancient principalities the chiefs whom we had restored, it would be necessary for us, however averse to the territorial acquisition within the hills, to retain such portions of the country as appeared best adopted for military positions and also calculated to indemnify the Government for the expenses of the military force, it was found necessary to retain in the hills."

The British Government, therefore, decided to retain a foothold in the strategic areas. It also decreed that all land, the ruling families of which had become extinct or the right to the possession of which was disputed between different states, should be also retained. The Maharaja of Patiala who rendered valuable service to the British in its operation against the Gurkhas, was rewarded with land in the neighbourhood of the area now comprising Simla. He was also allowed to purchase more land in the vicinity.

Thus two important factors weighed in favour of retaining the areas. As the 1887 *Imperial Gazeteer of India* noted, the area's proximity to Punjab and it being "an advantageous spot for recovery from the great chiefs of northern India" was one important factor. The other major factor, which the British were quick to notice and which paid them dividends in the years to come, was the docile nature of the local people, who were "simple-minded, orderly people, truthful in character and submissive to authority, so that they scarcely require to be ruled."

The British, however, did not pay immediate attention to the territory retained by them. We have the earliest account of the area from the diary of the Gerard brothers, who were both engaged in the survey of Sutlej river valley. In their notings dated August 30, 1817, they mentioned that Simla was "a middling-sized village where a fakir is situated to give water to the travellers . . . we encamped on the side of Jakhu, and had an extensive and beautiful prospect." It is also claimed that the area was first traversed by a British officer who recounted its beauty to his colleagues on his return.

But it was only in 1819 that the then Assistant Political Agent in hill states, Lieutenant Ross, set up the first British residence. It was a mere cottage of wood and thatch but it marked the beginning of a settlement which has left an indelible mark on the Indian history.

His successor, Lt. Charles Pratt Kennedy, erected the first *pucca* house in the area three years later. The researchers again have conflicting views on the precise house constructed by Lt. Kennedy. The town still has a building called 'Kennedy House' where certain government offices are now located. A doubt is expressed by some, whether this was the particular building, or an adjacent building which was gutted in a fire during the 1980's. Nevertheless, it is a near unanimous view that the first *pucca* house in Simla was erected in the vicinity of the area now occupied by the Himachal Legislative Assembly building.

The account of the salubrious surroundings and the invigorating climate of the area began attracting several British officers to the 'Kennedy House' during the scorching summer months. By 1826 the area acquired the shape of a settlement and some officers began spending their vacation in the area which, perhaps, revived memories of their country and its climate.

The European officers, most of whom were stated to be invalids or were on vacation, established themselves in the locality. They were either given free sites to construct houses or were allowed to stay in the mud and thatch houses if they so desired. The only condition imposed by the local ruler was that "they should refrain from the slaughter of kine and from the felling of trees unless with the previous permission of the proprietors of the land." The tales about the area began spreading far and wide and the then Governor-General Lord Amherst himself paid a visit in 1827 after completing the "progress" through the North-West and the triumphant ending of the Bharatpur campaign. He stayed in the 'Kennedy House' and to quote the *Gazeteer*, this visit was the "foundation of Simla's greatness." It was at the 'Kennedy House' that Lord Amherst said those famous words: "the Emperor of China and I govern half of the human race and yet we find time for breakfast !"

The following year Lord Comberemere, Commander-in-Chief of the British forces in India, visited Simla. Like Lord Amherst, he stayed in the 'Kennedy House', "a name given to two or three miserable shephards' huts" as Captain Mundy, the aide-de-camp to Lord Comberemere put it. The Commander-in-Chief, however, did not remain idle during his stay in the new settlement. He planned and got executed a three-mile road around the Jakhu hill. It was during his sojourn that he constructed a wooden bridge across a deep *nullah* below Jakhu. Though the bridge has been rebuilt at least twice, it still retains the name of its first builder. The bridge connected the main Simla to the Chhota Simla and is now one of the busiest thoroughfare. Undoubtedly, the construction of the wooden bridge by Lord Comberemere was one of the first developmental activities undertaken by the British in Simla.

An interesting description of the settlement at that time has been provided by Captain Mundy in a journal published in 1832. He wrote that the "climate of Simla soon became famous: invalids from plains resorted there, and built houses, instead of breaking up establishments and sailing for the Cape of Good Hope with little hope of reaching it; and finally Simla was rendered fashionable by the Governor-General Lord Amherst, who resided there with his family for several months and brought back to Calcutta rosy complexions and some beautiful drawings by Lady Sarah Amherst to attest the healthful and picturesque properties of the spot."

He has also given a witty description of his stay in tents: "I was completely drenched in my bed by the rain which fell in torrents; and the wind was so violent and the situation of our tent so exposed that I lay awake in momentary expectation of being blown away bodily into the valley 500 feet below . . . . I enjoyed, as stated above, a splendid view from my windows (I beg pardon, window), and the luxury of privacy, except at night when the rats sustained an eternal carnival, keeping me in much the same state as Whittington during his first week in London. I soon grew tired of bumping my head against the roof in pursuit of these four-footed pindarees, and at length became callous to their nocturnal orgies and kept a cat."

Lord Comberemere's visit followed more developmental activities in Simla. In anticipation of the visit of the then Governor-General, Lord William Bentinck, a house was constructed in 1829. He occupied the house on his visit during 1832. In 1829 itself, the appointment of Political Assistant at Sabathu was changed to that of Principal Assistant to the Resident of Delhi; and Captain Kennedy was the first incumbent to the new post. He was permitted to reside at Simla in view of the importance it was gaining.

The very next year, that is in 1830, the government decided that more land should be acquired in the vicinity of the settlement. It directed Major Kennedy to enter into negotiations with the chiefs of Keonthal and Patiala, who owned the land, to acquire land sufficient to form a station. He negotiated an exchange with the Rana of Keonthal for his portion of the Simla hills, comprising the 12 villages of Panjar, Sharrhan, Deberia, Phagli, Dalni, Kiar, Bamnoi, Pagawag, Dhar, Kanhlog, Kalhiana and Khalini. These villages yielded an annual income of Rs. 937 and in return handed over the Pargana of Rawin to the Rana of Keonthal which yielded a revenue of Rs. 1,289 per year. A portion of the Bharauli Pargana, consisting of Dhanoti, Kalawar and Dharol villages was handed over to the Maharaja of Patiala in exchange for Kainthu, Baghog, Cheog, and Aindari villages.

The *Simla District Gazetter* of 1888-89 mentions that the settlement grew with extraordinary rapidity. From 30 houses in 1830 it increased upward of 100 in 1841 and 290 in 1866. The number of occupied houses in 1881 was 1,141.

The first important political activity recorded in Simla is during the visit of Lord William Bentinck in 1832. He received a mission from Maharaja Ranjit Singh through which the famous meeting at Ropar was arranged. The same year Earl Dalhousie, who had succeeded Lord Comberemere as the Commander-in-Chief, came to Simla. From that year onwards, the Governor-Generals and Commanders-in-Chief almost regularly came to Simla during summer months. Yet another embassy from Maharaja Ranjit Singh to Lord Auckland arrived in 1838. The treaty of

1838 between the British and the Punjab Government and Shah Shuja was planned at Simla.

The 'Auckland House', as the Governor-General's house came to be known, was the scene of another important decision in 1838 which proved disastrous for the Britishers. It was here that the plan to invade Afghanistan was formulated by Lord Auckland and his Cabinet Secretaries. The Secretary's Lodge, the residence of the aide-de-camp of Lord Auckland, was the house from where the infamous "Simla Manifesto" declaring war with Afghanistan was issued.

Ironically, the decision to invade Afghanistan was criticised in the same house four years later and the "failure of Lord Auckland's policy in Afghanistan was acknowledged." The "altered intentions", as Edward J. Buck puts it, of the government were proclaimed by Lord Ellenborough "from the same building, in the same room, and on the very same day four years after the issue of the manifesto." The proclamation denounced in strong language the policy of his predecessor and expressed his willingness to "recognise any government approved by the Afghans themselves, which shall appear desirous and capable of maintaining friendly relations with neighbouring States."

Lord Auckland's sister Emily Eden has left a graphic account of those times. Referring to the Sikh embassy received by her brother in the building called 'Auckland House', she says that she was told that certain English ladies in Simla "would not dance because they had no idea of dancing before the natives." She felt that dancing in the presence of the natives should not be objectionable "as we invite 40 natives to each dance we give at Calcutta." Subsequently all the ladies, barring three, joined the dance and the Sikhs, "those poor ignorant creatures who are perfectly unconscious what a superior article the English woman is . . . . were all very quiet and well behaved."

Simla was attaining popularity day by day and each summer witnessed an added influx of those who found the area "good for liver" and "good for the soul" or an escape from the "dreadful plains" and to help the constitution of those who suffered from "too much East". As a coincidence, Queen Victoria ascended the

British Throne in 1837 and her tenure was marked by strict regimentation and court etiquette. A large number of young officers, who did not conform to discipline, were packed off to India as a punishment. To such officers, Simla offered an ideal setting with hardly any resrictions and a "home-like" atomsphere. The following years saw a bloom in the social life and an almost endless chain of fetes, picnics, games, balls, plays and sports. Vivid accounts have been left by some residents and visitors on the fun and frivolities of that period.

Simla also attracted some young British officers who sought to build up contacts with the high ups in the town. For this goal they tried to socialise with those in power to enhance their chance for better prospects. The town also became a haunt for young ladies for different reasons. Dr. Hoffmeister, physician to prince Waldemar of Prussia, who visited Simla in 1845, wrote in his account that "there was however by no means a lack of young ladies, for the kind and thoughtful relatives at Simla never fail to bring up from the plains everything in the shape of young and marriageable nieces and cousins; and here where so many agreeable officers are stationed for pleasure's sake alone, many a youthful pair are thrown together, and many a match is made." Indeed it became a resort, as the French Traveller M. Victor Jacquemont put it, "of the rich, the idle and the invalid."

In october 1851, the then Governor General Lord Dalhousie, who was known to be averse to spend time in balls, fetes and parties, wrote to a friend back home that "we have had a terrible fortnight of festivities. Balls without numbers, fancy fairs, plays, concerts, investitures—and every blank day filled up with a large dinner party. You may judge what this 'hill station' has grown to when I tell you that 460 invitations were issued for the last ball at Government House, and most of them came too!" He felt that the town has been greatly over-rated in climate and everything else, and would generally retire at a place several miles from Simla at Chini, much to the inconvenience of the officials.

He further wrote that there are too many festivities in Simla; "balls here, balls there, balls to the society, balls by the society, amateur plays, concerts, fancy fairs, investitures of the Bath and Co. and Co. I quite sigh for the quiet of Calcutta" and the Bishop of Calcutta was constrained to note that "during the season such amusements are carried to an excess and involve much that is questionable."

A Special Correspondent of the *Times*, Sir William Howard Russell, who visited Simla in 1857, exclaimed—"to taste such pleasures we must be sick, wounded, roasted and worn-out in the dreadful plains of India." The then Commander-in-Chief, General Napier, worried over the reputation the place was acquiring, curtailed the leave of officers and attempted to impose restrictions on visits to Simla. In return he was made the butt of ridicule by anonymous letter-writers in newspapers.

Annandale, a patch of table-land near a glen, became one of the favourite spots for picnics, fetes and sports. Like in most other matters, the various writers are divided over the origin of the name of the famous grounds. Some ascribe it to a girl named Anna who first visited the place, while others take the view that some officer named it so in memory of a similar place back home. Yet some other wrote that it was the name given by a British officer whose girl friend's name was Anna.

The first fancy fair was held in the grounds in September 1833 to raise funds for the establishment of a school for "native females" at Sabathu. The fairs became a regular feature and Annandale became the favourite spot for the merry makers. Edward J. Buck in his *Simla Past and Present* observes that "there is possibly no name connected with Simla which to thousands of Anglo-Indians, past and present, can revive more memories of a pleasant nature than the Annandale." It attained such an importance that the Viceregal dance in honour of the Queen's birth-day was "actually held at Annandale" on May 24, 1839.

Captain G.P. Thomas, who visited Simla in 1839, has written about the Simla society of those days. According to him Simla is "indifferent stupid for the first few weeks, for, despite the maxim that everybody knows everybody, nobody knows anybody for about that time, and society is accordingly as stiff and hollow, if not quite as deceptive as horse hair petticoat. But towards the end of the season, just when it is time perhaps to bid an eternal farewell people get up an eternal friendship, all becomes holiday costume;

and what with balls, races, picnics and exploring parties, we prove our belief, that it is the business of true wisdom to enjoy the present moment, and let care go hang herself in her garters. Then come on (or come off, which is it) at the same time, the races at Annandale, the race ball and the fancy fair."

While fun and frolic were the order of the day, some of the visitors and residents also began to promote art exhibitions and plays. Another aspect of such activities, besides a serious endeavour to promote entertainment, has been brought forth by Emily Eden who mentioned in her diary dated June 9, 1838 that she went to a play in "a sort of little theatre" but before the play could begin "the actors fell out". She stated that "one man took a fit of low spirits, and another who acted women's parts well, would not cut off his moustache, and another went off to shoot bears near the snowy range." Thus the play, which was supposed to be held in aid of poor people, could not be held.

For several years plays were held by amateurs in the Assembly rooms near the Lower Bazar. However in 1852, a part of the building collapsed and 'Abbevile' became the venue of plays for some years. Plays were also staged at the residences of the Viceroys and the Commanders-in-Chief.

The growing population and consequently the needs of the people contributed to the growth and development of the town. A large number of bungalows sprung up and the condition of roads was considerably improved. Besides the Lower Bazar, a big bazar was established at a rather flat land which was later converted into a ridge. The resourceful Indian businessmen, chiefly Soods and Parsis, opened shops and made arrangements for supplying provisions required by the residents and visitors. The Indians were, obviously, looked down upon and were barred from the area frequented by the Europeans. A large number of shops and business establishments were also opened by Europeans but we have an account of the bazar during those days which states that it "is thronged with natives, from the scarlet and golden messenger of the British Government to our old friends the Tibetans. . . within 20 yards is one of the grandest sights in the world. A splendid panorama of hill and valley, with the eternal snows as a background on one side, while on the other the view melts away

into the distant plains, across which the great Sutlej is seen like
a silver band. But to our brown friends such things possess no
attraction. The bustle, the closeness, smells, flies, pariah dogs,
unowned children of the kennel, and all the attractions of the
bazar are to them more pleasing than the majestic tranquility of
mountain and valley and far-off plain."

Initially, the shopkeepers, like the British visitors, came to
Simla only during the summer period and closed their establishments during the winters when the population of the town dwindl-
ed considerably. Some well-known traders from Delhi and Lahore
also opened branches of their shops in Simla but majority of the
shopkeepers were Soods who belonged to Kangra valley. The
Soods, whose contribution to the development of Simla has been
immense, set up business as retailers, wholesalers, commission
agents and money-lenders. They also grew up as a strong and well-
knit community. The more enterprising among them procured
wholesale goods from the plains and supplied commodities to the
bazars in the suburbs. Most of them purchased land to construct
shops which were mainly located in the Lower Bazar and the portion of land now called the Ridge.

In the *Journal of a Tour in India* during 1832, Captain Mundy
has described the Simla bazar of those days. He says that the bazar
"is proportionate to the necessities of its patrons, and forms a neat
little village, snugly situated under the shoulder of a lofty conical
mountain called Jako. . . . there are grain shops, butchers, tailors
and co. to meet the exigencies of the place."

Barring the bazars and trade, the town grew entirely on official
patronage. Lord Auckland's successors, Lord Ellenborough and
Lord Harding preferred to stay at the 'Auckland House' but Lord
Dalhousie decided to spend one season at the 'Strawberry Hill' and
the next two at the renovated 'Kennedy House'. Lord Canning who
visited Simla in 1860 preferred to stay at the 'Barnes Court' which
was for several years the residence of successive Commanders-in-
Chief. The first resident of the 'Barnes Court' was Sir Edward
Barnes and barring four of his successors, the others occupied this
house till 1860. Scores of other spacious houses were also constructed to accommodate the senior officers accompanying the

Governor-Generals and Commanders-in-Chief besides the Lieutenant Governor of Punjab. These houses bore typical English names.

The famous Christ Church, which stands majestically on the Ridge till date, was designed for the entire Christian population of Simla at that time. Its first corner-stone was laid by Rev. Daniel Wilson, Bishop of Calcutta, and Metropolitan of India on September 9, 1844.

Several roads were widened in the vicinity of the town following an injunction to the hill states to construct 12-foot wide roads. The road connecting the Chhota Simla was widened and the other roads in the town were "tolerably safe for the sober passengers" as Captain Mundy described them. The construction of the Hindustan-Tibet road was also taken up and a 560-feet tunnel was constructed beyond the Sanjauli bazar during 1851-52. According to Buck, "in its execution, indeed, it is recorded that some 10,000 prisoners and over 8,000 free labourers were employed."

The rather smooth social life in Simla was disrupted during 1857 when the first war of Indian Independence broke out. The tales of "mutiny" sent shivers up the spines of the Europeans in Simla. The news reached Simla on May 12, 1857. The different versions of the event at Simla can lead us to some conclusions. Towelle has given an account in his handbook about the panic in Simla but his description has been described as "exaggerated" as he was not in Simla during that period.

He has written that on May 11 "the storm broke out, and a panic seized the unprepared inhabitants. Hastily orders were issued, by some who took the command of affairs in hand, for all the ladies and children to assemble first at the Church and subsequently at the Simla Bank, in case a necessity arose to seek a place of refuge. Great was the confusion which ensued; on the signal agreed upon (the firing of two guns) being given, a few rolled up bundles of bedding and clothes, and hurried to the place of rendezvous. Some did not even wait to collect the necessary garments but started as they were, with alarm depicted on their countenances. Unfortunately there was no one to take the lead and restore any kind of order."

"The ladies were in hysterics, children crying, and the gentle-men hastily endeavouring to erect barricades on the top of the hill on which the Simla Bank, now the Grand Hotel, once stood. After a time the rumour came that the Gurkha regiments sta-tioned at Jutogh had mutinied, and that some of the Gurkhas were coming to 'loot' Simla. This made matters worse, and im-mediately not only was the Bank deserted, as it was supposed that it would be first place the mutineers would try to seize, but some went off by by-paths, avoiding the main raod, to Kussowlie and Dagshai to seek protection in the European barracks; some sought shelter in the territories of hills chiefs of the neighbourhood, others rushed into the interior of the hills, filling the dak bungalows on the road—all appeared to be bereft for the time of their senses. The scene that followed was so ludicrous, seeing the utter want of adequate cause of alarm, and shed so little glory on the courage of those in authority and of the inhabitants, Europeans as well as the natives, that the less written on the subject the better."

Commenting on the period after the "mutiny", he has written that "suffice it to say that in a few weeks order was restored, people returned to their houses, surprised to find them and their property intact, for notwithstanding the dire confusion, it was astonishing that no robberies took place, scarcely even a petty theft, though the opportunities for being unmindful of the laws of *meum et tuum* were so numerous, houses having been left open and unprotected, even keys and cash having been heedlessly for-gotten on tables and drawers. The cash in the Simla Bank was perhaps saved from being made away with by the simple fact of the secretary having the key of the strong room in his pocket when he, with others, left the bank to take care of itself."

The Special Correspondent of the *Times* William Howard Russell who visited Simla in the following year, has written that the Europeans in Simla seemed to be facing a real danger as the troops at Jutogh who "were in a state very little removed from open mutiny." He has written, obviously on the accounts he received during his visit, that soldiers looted the treasury at the neighbouring stations and it was providential that the soldiers at Jutogh were "restrained" from revolt. Depicting the scene at that time in Simla, he has written that "Simla was full of women, and men more timid than the women, and many bad characters were in the bazar ready for plunder and outrage if the troops broke out. A revolt on the very borders of Punjab might have roused the Sikhs beyond Lawrence's control, and then, indeed history would have had to philosophize over the fall of our Empire in India."

The Commander-in-Chief of the Army, General Anson, who was in Simla when the first war of Independence broke out, rushed to Delhi. However, he fell ill on the way and died before he could reach Delhi.

The account left by G.W. DeRhe Phillips, who was residing in Simla, when the news reached the town notes that there was marked panic among the European residents. But he has written that not everything was in disorder. He has stated that the then Deputy Commissioner, Lord William Hay who left for Jutogh, attempted to "reason" with the Gurkha soldiers stationed there. "Meanwhile, in consequences of positive intelligence reaching the station that the Gurkhas had broken out into mutiny and were coming up in to loot the place, a considerable number of citizens, in accordance with arrangements made the day before, assembled at the Bank under the command of Major General Nocholas Penny, for the purpose of making a stand, and here they remained until Lord William Hay came back from Jutogh late at night, and reported that the troops had returned to duty and advised those at the Bank to proceed to their house."

Phillips further stated that even after the announcement by Lord Hay many Europeans remained at the Bank and spent the night there. At the same time "a report quickly gained credence that Lord William had hinted it would be as well if everyone left Simla for a while, and accordingly on Saturday, the 16th May 1857 there was a considerable, but, considering the circumstances, a quiet and orderly exodus to Mashobra and the Junga State. A certain number of bolder spirits, however, steadily declined to leave until danger had really declared itself. There is no doubt that people living in Chhota Simla were at the outset informed that the Gurkhas had arrived in the main station and that they were in possession of the bazar. Hearing this, and finding their only road to the Bank was closed, almost all these residents dispersed down the *Khud* sides without further ado, and many of them suffered considerable hardships before returning." It was amongst these people that the so-called 'Simla panic' of May 1857 occurred, not amongst those who assembled at the Bank as is generally "but quite erroneously" supposed, according to Buck.

The "Mutiny Record Reports" contains a letter from Lord William Hay, Deputy Commissioner, Simla to Mr. G.G. Barnes, Commissioner and Superintendent, Ambala which is not only revealing but provides an insight into the attitude of the British towards their Indian subjects. In the letter dated February 6, 1858, Lord Hay has written that "the fearful intelligence from the plains, the very questionable fidelity of the Gurkhas, and the unprotected state of the station naturally produced the greatest alarm amongst the European residents and some of them early in the morning of the 14th May applied to Colonel Chester, Adjutant-General of the Army, and obtained an order for the Jutogh Magazine for a supply of muskets and ammunition, for the conveyance of which I was requested to make the necessary arrangements."

On reaching Jutogh on 15th morning the Deputy Commissioner wrote, "Just as I got about three quarters of a mile from the station, a most unexpected sound of shouting and violent altercation fell on my ears. I observed natives flying in every direction; some, chiefly coolies, to the top of the neighbouring heights; others, mostly *Bunias* and trade-people, towards Simla. I saw and heard quite enough to convince me that the Regiment had mutinied. While talking to the European residents in Simla who asked his opinion whether it was advisable to remain in the station, 'I said decidedly that implicit faith was not to be placed in the Regiment, and that, though I did not think there was ground to anticipate any immediate danger, I was of the opinion that it would be wise to withdraw the ladies.' " He further says "whether I was right or wrong in giving this advice I leave to others to decide. Of one thing I am quite certain, namely, that nothing I could say or do would have prevailed to stop or in anyway check the flight of the Europeans from Simla."

He further writes, "some took refuge at Junga, the residence of Rana of Keonthal, others with the Thakurs of Kotee or Bulsum;

while the remainder sought safety in the hill cantonments of Dugshai, Subathoo and Kussolie. In the hurry of the moment few provided themselves suitable means of conveyance or even with a small stock of provisions, consequently all were exposed to annoyances and privations; many underwent great hardships, while a few went with severe injuries. Happily they experienced much kindness at the hands of hill chief; and, as Gurkhas shortly after marched for the plains. Confidence was gradually restored and the inconveniences to which all had been more or less subjected were soon forgotten."

Unfortunately, no written account of the contemporary times by the Indians is available. In fact there is hardly any account left by any Indian throughout the 19th century and Simla of those days can mainly be seen from the tinted glasses of the Europeans. Their notings, however, mention that the local population of Indians, chiefly constituting of traders and government officials, largely remained unaffected. Some of the neighbouring chieftains actually provided protection to the fleeing Europeans. The *Simla District Gazeteer of 1888-89* notes that the Rana of Keonthal rendered "good service during the mutiny" and his rank of Rana was raised to the higher rank of Raja in 1857 soon after the happenings at Simla had ended.

Thus though the reports of the first war of Indian Independence created panic among the European residents of Simla which was largely imaginary, the town remained more or less unaffected. While it proved "safe" from the British point of view, they also realised its strategic location to keep a close eye on Punjab. The cantonments built at strategic points before the annexation of Punjab provided a protective ring around Simla. Another argument in favour of permanently locating the summer capital of the Raj at Simla was that it was located in the centre of the then British empire.

But a decision to convert Simla into the summer capital was not taken immediately after 1857. The first Viceroy Lord Canning spent some time in Simla but he did not appear in favour of shifting the summer capital to the town. His wife found the "beauty of this place very questionable; and it is such a sea of hill tops and the snowy mountains are so far off and the dryness makes it all look wintry."

To John Lawrence goes the credit of the decision to shift the summer capital of the Raj to Simla. He unexpectedly was appointed the Viceroy in 1863 after the sudden death of Lord Elgin. He very strongly favoured the shifting of the summer capital to Simla and wrote to the Secretary of State that "of all the hill stations Simla seems to me the best for the Supreme Government. Here you are with one foot, I may say, in the Punjub and another in the North West Provinces. Here you are among a docile population and yet near enough to influence Oudh. Around you, in a word, are all the war-like races of India, all those on whose character and power our hold in India, exclusive of our own countrymen, depends . . . . now a days you have no large native army to fear. What you have on this side of India, you have mainly around and about you, so that your Governor-General, if he has any discernment, is well placed to perceive the first signs of danger and is then able to apply a remedy."

He doggedly pursued his desire to shift summer capital to Simla, partly also due to his health problem but more so because he seemed convinced that Simla is the ideal place for the summer capital. He again wrote to the Secretary of State that "the work of government is probably treble, possibly quadruple what it was 20 years ago, and it is, for the most part, of a very difficult nature. Neither your Governor-General nor his Council could really do it in the hot weather of Calcutta. At the very best they would work at half the speed." He asserted that the government shall do "more work in Simla in one day than what it could do in five days at Calcutta."

2
The Zenith
1861–1920

The intense persuasion of Lawrence paid dividends and the Secretary of State, Sir Charles Wood, wrote back to him that "with or without, your Council, you are quite welcome to be away from Calcutta for six months, and therefore you may set your mind quite at ease on that point. If you like next summer to go and see Madras and the Neilgherries, and put some life into their proceedings, or visit Darjeeling, and our new enemies in Bhutan, or go to Simla again, I have no objection."

It is quite clear from the communication that the British Government had not decided that Simla would be made the summer capital of the Indian Empire. Lawrence was simply given the option but as it turned out, Simla was actually made the summer capital and till the second decade of the next century it remained more important than even Calcutta or Delhi. Since no period was fixed for the "exodus" of the government to and from Simla, the dates were fixed at the convenience of successive Viceroys. In fact, during the initial period, partly due to bad transportation system, the government remained absent from Calcutta for periods ranging upto eight months each year.

The four decades of virtual rule from Simla saw several major developments which directed the course of Indian history. This was the place from where the "white gods looked down upon the lesser beings who inhabited the plains of Hindustan from their Mount Olympus in the western Himalayas", as Dr. M.S. Randhawa put in his *Travels in the Western Himalayas*. Millions of people, extending from Red Sea on the one side and Bhutan on the other, were governed by what transpired at Simla between the people who ruled and made history.

Simla consequently became the centre of major activities, both political and social. The prophetic words of Captain Mundy came true. He had written in 1828 that "I cannot doubt but that Simla will rise in importance every year as it becomes better known" and had asserted that it would "induce" the Governor-Generals and Commanders-in-Chief to resort in the hill town during the hot weather. In his *Twenty One Days in India*, George Aberigh-Mackay has in a satirical tone written that the Viceregal office at Simla was the "sensorium of the empire; it is the seat of thought, it is the abode of moral responsibility. What famines, what battles, what excursions of pleasure, what banquets and pageants, what concepts of change have sprung into life here! every pigeon-hole contains a potential revolution; every office box cradles the embryo of a war or death, what shocks and vibrations, what deadly thrills does this thunder cloud office transmit to far away provinces lying beyond rising and setting suns."

What started as a trickle soon after the war with the Gurkhas in 1815-16, turned into a torrent with the annual shifting of the government offices to Simla. While in 1864, 107 clerks travelled with the government from Calcutta to Simla, their number rose to 217 in 1873 and 376 in 1889 and upto 641 in 1905. The actual strength of officials and servants accompanying the government was more than thrice that number per year. The decision to shift the Army Headquarters from Calcutta permanently to Simla in 1864 contributed to the rising population of Simla. Several other offices attached to the Army Headquarters, including those of the Director-General and Examiner of Military Accounts, the Indian Medical Service, the Director-General of Ordnances and the Army Removal Department, were also shifted to Simla. These were followed by offices of the Criminal Investigation Department, the Meteorological Department and the Sanitary Department in 1884.

The offices of the Punjab Government were also shifted for about five months each year from 1871 to 1873. From 1876 it became an annual practice though the Punjab Government continued to function mainly from Lahore. Thus besides the migratory population, the town absorbed a large number of officials and their families who were stationed at Simla throughout the year. Besides the officials and the clerks, who accompanied the government, an almost endless stream of officials and visitors poured into Simla during each summer. There were "men so tremendous in their own spheres" who brought crates full of "dispatch boxes" to be cleared during their sojourn in the summer capital.

The European town, nestling in the serene atmosphere of the Himalayas, turned into one of the busiest places in the country. In his *Good-bye India*, Sir Henry Sharp has written "below that artificial and peaceful surface there lies a stern reality, an undertone of busy activity. For, here is the Olympus where the gods, when they did not descend to Calcutta or Delhi, sat (and, I presume, still do less often sit) not careless of mankind but worrying a good deal about the welfare of the one-fifth of the human race, declared or composed wars, issued fiats for enthronements and dis-crownments. And, amid this hum of public affairs, some folk have been unkind enough to say they could not sleep (all) nights by reason of the sound of the grindings of private axes."

The four decades left many important landmarks including the decisions taken about Afghanistan and the famous Simla conference of 1873. From the Indian nationalist point of view these were some of the most important years for the initial steps towards the independence. Simla can claim the credit for being the place where the Indian National Congress was conceived and where the idea of forming the Muslim League gained ground. Both the organisations were to play a pivotal role in the years to come.

It was in 1873 that Sayyid Nur Mohammad, an envoy of the Amir Sher Ali of Afghanistan arrived at Simla to hold discussions with the then Viceroy, Lord Northbrook. It was certainly a critical phase in the Amir's relations with the British. The Amir had wanted to obtain a definite and practical British protection in the face of growing influence and unsought patronage of the Russians. It is believed that the envoy from the Amir requested for a complete alliance with the British. Lord Northbrook sent his recommendations to the Liberal Government in England and suggested that Afghanistan should be provided money, arms and even troops in case of an invasion on Afghanistan. The Government in England, however, did not accept the suggestion of the Viceroy which later led to serious consequences. The envoy of the Amir left merely with an assurance of "friendly neutrality" of the Government of India. Later, however, Disraeli took over the office in England and gave up Gladstone's policy of "masterly inactivity" and pursued the "forward policy" in relation to Afghanistan.

Later during the tenure of Lord Lytton, another envoy of the Amir met the Viceroy at Simla regarding the proposal to send a British envoy to Kabul to which Sher Ali now had an objection. It was decided to hold a conference at Peshawar to clinch the issue. A string of events later culminated in the declaration of a bloody war against Afghanistan in 1878.

Simla was also the scene of the historically very important tripartite conference in which the British, the Chinese and the Tibetans participated during 1913-14. China was obviously fearing that the British may hold direct negotiations with Tibet and the Chinese were also disturbed by the success of Russians in Mongolia. Initially they were reluctant to hold the discussions in India. They would have preferred London or Peking and were not in favour of meeting the Tibetans on the same footing. The British Government was represented by Sir Henry Macmohan and Sir Charles Bell while China was represented by Ivan Chen and Tibet by Lonchen Shatra. The Tibetans wanted an acknowledgement of their independence and the acceptance of a frontier with China. The Chinese, claimed sovereignty over Tibet and backed their claim by pointing out that Tibet was conquered by Chengez Khan. They demanded that Tibet should be declared an integral part of China. Thus there were "two widely divergent extremes" as H.E. Richardson described it and Sir Macmohan's role was that of a "mediator trying to find some common ground" between the two.

The various proposals put forward during the six-month long negotiations led to a draft tripartite convention document. The Chinese had been pressing for more concessions and, later, the Chinese Government declined to accept the proposals. Richardson notes that "strenuous efforts were made by Macmohan to save the conference from failure." The Chinese did not relent, the conference was wound up and in 1914 Macmohan signed a convention with the Tibetan representative. The main Chinese objection was related to the proposed boundaries between China and Tibet northward from the Burmese border. The direct negotiations between the British and the Tibet also resulted in what is now known as the 'Macmohan Line' which was fixed roughly along the Himalayas from the north-east corner of Bhutan to the Isu Razi Pass in the north of Burma. The question has remained unresolved till date.

While the British were still engaged in expansion and consolidation of their Empire, the political consciousness in India was rising slowly but surely. The last two decades of the 19th century were quite important in this context. It was at Simla during that period that the Indian National Congress, which was later to spearhead the struggle for freedom of the country, was conceived and given a practical shape. Though several groups had sprung up in favour of the nationalist movement, it was left to Allen Octavian Hume, a former British officer, to do the all important "linking in". To most of his countrymen and to many Indians, he remained an enigma but he was the man who called out:

"Sons of Ind, why sit ye idle,
Wait ye for some deva's aid ?
Buckle to, be up and doing
Nations by themselves are made"

In 1883 Hume addressed an open letter to the graduates of the Calcutta University urging them to devote themselves earnestly and unselfishly to the cause of the progress of the country with a view to secure a greater freedom for the Indians. He also took up the cause of Indians with successive Viceroys. Both Lord Northbrook and his successor Lord Lytton did not see eye to eye with Hume. Infact, to get rid of him, Lord Lytton abolished the Department of Agriculture, Revenue and Commerce which he was heading. Hume resigned from the service at the age of 50 and settled at the 'Rotheny Castle' at Simla which he had purchased earlier.

The 'Rotheny Castle' was the house from where Hume mooted the idea of forming a cohesive organisation. Lord Lytton's successor Lord Ripon seemed more appreciative of Hume's ideas. Thus a "conspiracy", as Prof. S.R. Mehrotra, a noted historian who has done considerable research on the Indian National Congress likes to call it, between 'Peterhoff' (the Viceroy's residence) and the 'Rotheny Castle' paved the way for a broad-based Indian organisation.

In his book *The Emergence of the Indian National Congress*, Prof. Mehrotra clearly states that "Hume was not the first person either to conceive the idea of an All India political organisation, or to attempt to realise it but his was the authority, the energy and the organisational skill that accomplished the seemingly impossible." In fact, the first known modern political organisation, the Bengal Land-holders' Society, was established in 1838 and several other organisations were formed later.

Hume earnestly set about his task in 1884. His biographer William Wadderburn has written that "the state of things at the end of Lord Lytton's reign was bordering upon a revolution." Some critics believe that Hume was keen to provide a "safety valve" for the growing Indian nationalist feelings while some others assert that he unconsciously feared the repetition of the events that had taken place in 1857.

Hume wrote numerous letters from 'Rotheny Castle' and toured large parts of the country in preparation for holding a joint meeting at Pune by the end of 1885. However, the venue of the conference had to be changed to Bombay in the wake of an outbreak of cholera at Pune. While most of the 72 delegates at the first session of the Congress did not know each other; Hume knew them all. He continued working for the organisation in an effort to strengthen it. He left India in 1892 but returned two years later to attend the Lahore session. Back in England he continued to work for the Congress till his death in 1912 at the age of 83. By that time the Congress had come of age.

Michael Edwards has written in his *Bound to Exile* that "most Anglo-Indians regarded Hume's foundation of the Indian National Congress as just another of the eccentricities with which Simla abounded. Some of these were forgivable; others were not."

But for the Indians his contribution was immense and invaluable despite the fact that the present Congress leaders have sought to turn a blind eye on his role to form the organisation. Even his

house, 'Rotheny Castle' at Simla has been allowed to be converted into a luxury hotel, ironically, during the centenary year of the
Congress. The gratitude of the nation, however, is reflected in an
editorial published in *The Tribune* dated March 31, 1894 on the
occasion of his farewell from India: "All India was present in spirit at the great meeting in which Bombay bade farewell to Mr.
Hume. The very thought of saying good-bye to the man to whom,
more than to anyone else, India owes her reawakening, is sadden-
ing; and no wonder that the eyes of even the hardest-headed businessmen in the assembly were moist when Mr. Hume had finished his speech—probably his last public utterance in this country.
The love and the feeling of reverence of young India towards Mr.
Hume are things of which all Englishmen should feel proud if
they view them in their true light. Englishmen have done deeds
of romantic valour and have earned imperishable renown by un-
paralleled achievements in many directions, but no other Englishman, in our humble opinion, can show a record of work equal to
that of Mr. Hume in his own sphere. A magician who takes some
dry bones, and collecting them in a heap sprinkles water over
them and makes them instinct with life, does not do a more won-
derful thing than Mr. Hume had done. He had literally put life into
dead bones; has not only arrested the downward course of our
unhappy people, but has dragged them into the path of progress
and has been leading them onwards towards a glorious destiny".

Hume was given a loud and warm applause when he concluded his speech by saying that "there was no nation on the face of
Earth that could rival India in its kindness and courtesy" and he
expressed the hope that when the seed, he had helped to sow,
yielded its harvest, India's sons would accord this epitaph graven
not in bronze or marble, but written in loving word: "He laboured zealously for India's cause and if he sometimes erred, he greatly loved us".

While Simla has an important place in the birth of the Indian
National Congress, it was also the venue where the "turning
point" in the history of the formation of the Muslim League was
reached. The League, which was the mouth-piece of the Muslims
of India during the nationalist movement, partly owes its origin
and formation after a delegation of Muslims had met the Viceroy

Lord Minto at Simla. Sir George Dunbar in his *History of India* says that the Viceroy made the "first official acknowledgement of the Moslem claim for separate representation" while replying to a deputation led by Agha Khan III at Simla in 1906. Some of the critics feel that the establishment of the Muslim League was indirectly encouraged by Lord Minto who "instigated" the Muslims against the Hindu-dominated Congress.

The Pakistan Historical Society Publication, *A History of the Freedom Movement* (vol III, part I) has described at length the formation of the Muslim League. It has stated that the Secretary of State for India, John Morely, while delivering his budget speech in 1906 spoke of some constitutional reforms. Nawab Mohsin-ul-Mulk, who was in Bombay, felt concerned about the impact of the reforms on Muslims. Accordingly an appointment was fixed with the Viceroy at Simla and Agha Khan III was nominated to head the deputation. The deputation was received by the Viceroy on October 1, 1906 at the Viceregal Lodge. A memorandum submitted to the Viceroy read that, "it is true that many of our aims and interests are common with those of our Hindu brethren, and it shall always be a source of pleasure and satisfaction for us that there should be in the Councils competent men, irrespective of creed and community, who can protect these aims and interests. Nevertheless, it cannot be denied that from the national point of view, we Muslims form a separate body which is quite distinct from the Hindus." The deputation also demanded that the electoral system for the elected bodies should be such as to provide the right to Muslims to elect their own representatives from special constituencies. They said that keeping in view their historical importance and political position, the Muslims should be given more seats than are warranted by their population. They also demanded appointments to gazetted and non-gazetted positions in same proportion and adequate representation in the judiciary.

Lord Minto in his reply said, "for the present I assure you that the Muslims of India can rest assured that so long as I have anything to do with the governance of this country, their rights and interests will receive the fullest consideration. You and all the people of India can trust that as the British Government in the past has had the privilege of treating with consideration and regards

the various creeds and communities which compose the population of India, so it always be." His remark which really proved
the *fait accompli* for the Muslim League was: "I am as firmly
convinced as I believe you, to be that any electoral representation
in India would be doomed to mischievous failure which aimed at
granting a personal enfranchisement, regardless of the beliefs and
traditions of the communities composing the population of this
continent".

Subsequently the Muslim League was formally launched on
December 30, 1906 at an All India Conference of the Muslims at
Dhaka.

While Simla was witness to events of such import, it also attracted the attention of the rulers for development. Being the summer seat of the Imperial Government it quite naturally received a
larger share of funds for improvement and general development.

A good transportation and communication system was the
first requirement for the government which spent over half the
year at Simla. Till 1856, when the Cart Road from Kalka to Simla
was completed, the mode of transportation was mules and hor-
ses. The luggage was hauled up by the local people and at times,
porters had to be forcibly brought from distant places in view of
the shortage of man-power. They were paid very poorly and were
weaned away from their occupations, including farming, to carry
the luggage of the white "sahibs". The completion of the Cart
Road enabled the plying of *jampans*, a sedan chair, which was
carried by porters. The annual move to Simla, says Ian Stephens,
was "romantic but rather horrifying." He further wrote: "the
memory that sticks in my mind is of those coolies pulling and
humping terribly heavy loads on their backs up-hill slopes." The
"exodus" involved tonnes of baggage, heaps of files and dispatch
boxes besides the families of the officials. As Andrew Wilson described the event: "there were colonels and clerks of departments
and other men so tremendous in their spheres. Assistant Deputy
Commissioners, still relatively unburdened with the cares of
highest office cantering lightly along parapet-less roads skirting
precipices" and the "ton weight of a post office official requiring
20 groaning coolies to carry him."

The road was still quite narrow and prone to landslides. In fact the shopkeepers at Simla charged extra from customers to cover the risk of damage to the goods brought from Kalka. With the growing importance of the town, the road was widened and *tongas* were introduced. The *tonga* service was introduced by Mr. George Law who had got the idea from a similar service in the Central Province. The service for mail and passengers was conducted efficiently under the supervision of Rai Bahadur Dowlat Ram.

The *tonga* service was initially provided by private owners. The government took over the service in two stages and established its total control in 1881.

Though the service proved very useful, the government was keen to introduce the railway from Kalka to Simla. In fact, a suggestion was mooted way back in 1847 and initial plan was drawn but nothing further was done. The "exodus" to and from Simla made it imperative that the railway be introduced. It was by no means an easy job and the laying of railway lines involved great hazards. Lord Curzon, the then Viceroy took active interest in its completion which was carried out under the supervision of the Chief Engineer, Mr. H.S. Harington. The laying of the railway line, which is about 60 miles in length, involved the construction of 103 tunnels aggregating about five miles. The longest tunnel was the 'Barog tunnel', being 1143.61 metres in length. The railway line was opened for goods traffic on March 31, 1891 and the first passenger train was flagged off only on November 9, 1903.

The railway line between Kalka and Simla did not prove to be a financial success during the initial years. It was constructed at a cost of $ 4,00,000 by the Delhi-Umballa Company and partly through advances amounting to Rs. 1,16,47,512 from the government. The sanctioned cost for the railway line was Rs. 86,78,500 but the actual cost turned out to be Rs. 1,71,07,748. The government took over the railway line with effect from January 1, 1906.

The opening of the railway line to Simla resulted in a sudden increase in its population. The increase before and after 1891, even though the line had not been thrown open for passenger traffic, was 24 per cent. While during the 1889 enumeration, the population of the town was 24,179; the census in 1898 put the population at 30,405. The Municipal Committee, however, was of the opinion that the population figures of 1898 census were "below the mark" as it was not undertaken during the most crowded period of the year. Also the census had not reflected the floating population which was quite considerable during those days.

The increase in the population necessitated more and better civic amenities. Credit must be given to the British rulers who meticulously planned and executed the projects. It would be justified to go into details of some of the projects if one wishes to compare the formulation and execution of some of such schemes in the present times. A better communication between different parts of Simla through a road network was apparently given a priority. Several new areas were developed and connected with new roads. The improvements on the existing roads were also undertaken to make them fit for the plying of *tongas* to make way for the "coolies that infest" the main roads. The roads which were improved included the one around 'Kelston' on the east side, Chaura Maidan to Summer Hill and 'Ridgewood Place' to Forest Hill. Perhaps the most important of the roads which were widened and improved at that time was below the north side of the Ridge passing below the Lakkar Bazar and 'Blessington' (then known as the Lovers' walk) which connected the Kaithu bazar and which is now known as the Circular Road. It was further extended to the 'Kennedy House' on one side and Annandale on the other.

It was proposed to construct, according to the report of the Simla Extension Committee, 1898, another road from the Church to the Convent, running parallel with the Mall, but at a higher elevation around the Jakhu hill. The road was expected to be not only "a convenience to residents of the houses above the Church and Lowrie's hotel, but (to) open up building sites in the 'Barnes Court' estate and be an addition to the pleasant rides the station affords." The road is now known as the Forest Road. The report mentions that a third road that "would be a great convenience is the one starting from under the old Bandstand passing below Glenarm through Bairdville and the Portmore estate joining the Mall again just short of the Chhota Simla bazar." Among other proposed new roads were Belvedere to Bharari, Bonnie Moon-Bothwell to the Mall and from 'Blessington' to Annandale. Later, during 1914, it was decided to convert the "coolie and mule" road from Main bazar to the Chhota Simla which was actually an extension of the Mall road and is now one of the most busy thoroughfares.

Likewise, roads connecting the other towns in the region were also constructed. The 1898 Simla Extension Committee report notes that "with better communication with the trans-Sutlej States of Mandi and Suket and a further extension of the Mashobra suburb it may be necessary to make a Cart Road from Mashobra to Naldera and, in that case, the link from the Lakkar Bazar to Mashobra could easily be made, which would give uninterrupted communication for carts from Naldera to the hearts of Simla." It was designed to reduce the cost of commodities brought from those areas as also to relieve the congestion of traffic on the Mall.

Besides the roads, the local authorities paid earnest attention to the availability of water for the growing number of residents. The huge reservoir under the Ridge was constructed in 1880. For more than a hundred years now, the reservoir is the main source of supply to the Simla residents and the improvements made in the water supply system since then have been grossly inadequate. The report of the Simla Water Works Committee, 1904, gives in detail the water supply situation at that time. It points out that prior to 1880, the only source for the supply of water to the residents was through *baolis* or natural water springs. It says that "in 1880, the upper gravitation line was opened with the Church reservoir which holds 1,200,000 gallons, and two years later, the Sanjauli reservoir was added which contains 1,800,000 gallons." A third reservoir was constructed at Saog by 1904 and the cost of these reservoirs was Rs. 6,06,000. One of the biggest and powerful pumping engines was installed which has also been working satisfactorily for over 100 years now.

It is interesting to note the estimate of water requirements, as prepared by the Municipal Committee, separately for the European and the Indian residents. The report contains a chart showing that the water requirement for the 4,000 Europeans at 25 gallons per head was 1,00,000 gallons while for the "natives", the water requirement was five gallons per head and totalled 1,80,000 gallons. Flush latrines were provided exclusively for the Europeans while the Indians were only provided dry latrines. The report goes on to say that the requirement for the sanitary purposes was 1,12,000 gallons while for watering of roads (twice a day), the requirement was 30,000 gallons. It was estimated that building operations and animals would require 10,000 gallons while the railways would consume 5,000 gallons of water.

It was stressed that the supply of water can "be still husbanded and economised" if greater attention is paid to the stoppage of leakage and wastage. The then Commissioner of the Simla Municipal Committee had advocated compulsory storage of rain water for non-drinking purposes and had said that "even legal authority should be taken to compel" the residents to store rain water. The Committee expressed its total support for the suggestion and noted that the sooner it is done the better. The severe shortage of water in 1903, which was an exceptionally dry year, led to severe criticism of the water supply system and also to its repraisal. A Rs. 25-lakh scheme was mooted by one Major General Beresford and Mr. Pook for the construction of water lines and pumping of water from the Sutlej river. The scheme, however, did not find favour with the Simla Water Works Committee. In its report submitted in 1904, it said "we regret that we have been obliged to condemn so unreservedly a scheme on which its joint authors have laboured with some trouble, but so many of their statements are misleading and their figures are so very unreliable that we feel bound to speak decisively and to say that, though from an engineering point of view, the scheme may be feasible with extensive modifications, its original cost, high maintenance charges, and the enormous sacrifice of power it entails, put it quite out of court as a practical solution of the problem of how best the existing water supply of Simla may be extended."

Interestingly, the scheme is now being revived and its estimated cost has jumped from Rs. 25 lakhs then to Rs. 35 crores now.

The oil lighting of Simla was also gradually replaced with electric lighting. It is believed that the first electricity system was provided in the Viceregal Lodge at Simla in 1888 and about a

thousand lamps, mainly of 16 candle-power capacity, were installed in the Lodge and its compound. Lady Dufferin was obviously
thrilled with the electricity system and wrote that it "certainly is
very good, and the lighting up and putting out of the lamps is
so simple that it is quite a pleasure to go round one's room
touching a button here and there and to experiment with various
amounts of light."

Initially only public buildings were provided electricity. Besides
the Viceregal Lodge, the others were Barnes Court, the United
Services Club, Snowdon, Town Hall and the Government Press
which were provided electricity generated by steam power. These
were followed by street lighting. As late as 1904 the residents were
sceptic about getting private electricity connections. The Simla
Water Works Committee in its report in 1904 points out that
"private lighting will come on gradually and the number of houses
connected will probably be small for the first year or two, as the
first cost of fitting up houses will deter landlords from making a
start, and many will prefer to wait till they see that the public
lighting is a success and the power supply thoroughly reliable."

The increased power supply by the second decade of this century prompted the Simla Improvement Committee to recommend
in 1914, "as feasible and useful proposal" to instal a lift from the
Phagli road to the vicinity of the 'Gorton Castle' where the Imperial Government's Secretariat was located. The report also said
that "a lift from Annandale to the Mall we consider of such
doubtful feasibility and utility that we do not recommend its further consideration." However, the Committee recommended that
a lift from the Nabha Estate to the Mall road should be constructed but none of the two recommendations was executed.
Similar was the fate of a proposal to run electric tramways on the
Mall. The Committee was of the view that it would not pay a
good dividend.

There was also proposal to introduce electricity driven motors
on the 20 miles of roads around Simla. The Committee was of the
opinion that there is "considerable scope" for such a proposal.
Mr. J.W. Mears, Electrical Adviser to the Government of India
prepared an exhaustive scheme on electric tramway, rail-less trac-
tion and self-contained cars. However, he added that from a

commercial point of view none of the three modes was feasible. He rather advocated the introduction of motor rickshaw which could be operated by battery.

Simla also claims credit for the installation of one of the first automatic telephone exchanges in the country. The exchange was installed at the Central Telegraphic Office building. It had a capacity of 2000 lines and proved a boon to the government. Over the years, the exchange was connected to Calcutta, Delhi, Bombay and Lahore. Then in the 1930s it was also connected to England and the then Viceroy was the first person to talk from India to England. Improvements were made in the exchange from time to time and by 1951, the old exchange had been more or less replaced. The telegraph services were also subsequently improved and the *tonga* mail service was abolished soon after the goods train began to journey from Kalka to Simla.

The ever-growing population of the summer capital of India also led to a focus on the sewerage system of the town. The uncertainty about the availability of sufficient water in Simla had led to a certain bit of complacency for improvement in the sewerage system. The plans for augmentation of water supply schemes led to proposals to improve the sewerage system. Till about 1898 the sewerage system consisted only of four collecting tanks on the south side of the hill.

The Simla Extension Committee, realising the practical difficulty admitted that "when it is remembered that there is no main for all the north side of the hill, and that the liquid and solid sewage of every house, even from far distant Summer Hill and the back of Jakko has to be carried to these tanks, it is easy to understand how, notwithstanding the employment of an army of sweepers under liberal supervision, both Europeans and Natives, the carrying work is shirked as described by the civil surgeons, and the contents of the buckets only too often thrown down some out-of-the-way ravine".

The Committee suggested that the best practical remedy for such state of things was to construct more soil tanks so that every house in the town could have a tank at a reasonable distance. It proposed using the water from local springs and rain water for flushing purposes. The Committee also foresaw the future needs and suggested the construction of a sewage farm spread over an area of 50 acres.

It may sound ironic that while the modern day Simla does not have any incinerator, not even in the hospitals, the destruction of rubbish was carried out nearly a hundred years ago by incinerators in the town. The Committee, giving its report in 1950, said that the number of incinerators "should be increased at once from eight to twelve" as its members had found rubbish still thrown in the valleys in some parts of the town, particularly, Chhota Simla. The Committee endorsed a proposal for the erection of a "large incinerator of modern pattern" to consume rubbish from the Burra Bazar "without nuisance and to generate steam power or electricity for some useful purpose from the heat evolved."

A review of the sewage system was taken up in 1914 and it was found that "the present system of hand carriage and pail depots for the disposal of sewage in Simla is the cause of many nuisances and dangers" and the report of the Simla Improvement Committee in 1914 suggested that the Municipality should construct sewage mains so that these are within 100 feet of the latrine of each private compound and "that each private owner should provide and bear the cost of the flush latrine and the 100 feet connection." The Committee also suggested that sanction for the construction of new houses should be provided only if provision has been made for flush latrines and the existing houses should also be provided with flush latrines.

The growing prosperity of the town was also reflected in the large number of shops and the crowded bazars. Besides a large number of shops opened by the Europeans to deal mainly with the needs of the European residents, the bazars were crammed with shops opened by Soods, Parsis and others who were having a hey-day while Simla's population rose steeply. But obviously the rulers did not devote themselves to the improvement and development of bazar except the Mall road. Rudyard Kipling, who visited Simla during 1880s has described the Lower Bazar in his own inimitable style: "the crowded rabbit-warren that climbs up from the valley to the Town Hall at an angle of 45°. The man that knows his way there can defy all the police of India's summer capital; so cunningly does verandah communicates with verandah, alley-way with alley-way and bolt-hole with bolt-hole." He has also provided description of some shops particularly of a curio dealer, the famous "Lurgan Sahib".

Though the number of shops and buildings had not greatly increased till the turn of the century, the accommodation was vastly increased by constructing additional storeys, additional rooms and glazing verandahs. The Simla Extension Committee favoured that "no further extension, as distinguished from mere internal improvements in existing houses, should be allowed in the main, Lakkar and Kaithu bazars." The Committee suggested that the Boileauganj and Chhota Simla should be expanded and a new bazar be developed near the Railway Station.

The Ridge *Maidan*, one of the favourite spots for the residents and tourists and the scene of important official functions now, was lined with shops on either sides before a fire broke out in the bazar in 1875. It was then known as the 'Upper Bazar'. It contained a large number of shops owned by the Indians and some by the Europeans besides the police station. The gutted shops were not allowed to be re-built and the Simla Municipality gave alternative sites to the shopkeepers. To quote Edward J. Buck, "the Municipality wisely prohibited rebuilding, compensated proprietors for their lost sites, levelled down the crest of the road, and planted the flourishing copse now existing between the Town Hall and the Church. Later, when the construction of the Town Hall was decided upon, the Upper road was gallaried out, the result being the fine open Ridge now enjoyed by the inhabitants of the town." He goes on to mention that "fire has undoubtedly been answerable from time to time for marked improvements on the upper Mall, and many people wonder that the crowded native bazar of wooden houses has hitherto escaped destruction." Fortunately till the writing of these lines, the Lower Bazar, as crowded as ever, has remained safe. On the other hand, several old buildings, including some on the Mall and the Viceroy's residence, the 'Peterhoff', have been gutted over the years. Fire does remain a major hazard till date.

While Simla, unlike any other big town in the country, owes its existence solely to the British, its bazars provided them the main difference from their own country. Indeed the traders and the shopkeepers have played a major role in the development and in sustaining the town. It does seem curious that while the British rulers planned everything in meticulous detail, they left the bazar to itself which resulted in a haphazard construction.

They did realise it but perhaps it was too late. In fact the Simla Improvement Committee report of 1914 makes a candid confession that "no control was exercised in the past over the growth of these collection of buildings, which are in great part unfit for human habitation, both on account of their structural defects, and of their over-crowded position. Moreover, no adequate provision has been made to cope with the rapid increase in the Indian population; conditions, already bad, have been gravely aggravated; and it is impossible to enforce rules against over-crowding until accommodation can be provided elsewhere for the displaced population. Insanitary conditions in certain localities rival those in the worst slums in cities in the plains, and constantly one of the most difficult problems for the local Municipality."

It is also interesting to note that Committee on Simla Improvement in 1907 had recommended that the Lakkar Bazar should be demolished and the shopkeepers given alternative sites. The Committee had described the bazar as "an excrescence on the European quarter." Endorsing the suggestion of the Committee, the 1914 Committee stressed that it needs radical treatment and it should be acquired and demolished. As such, the report said, the bazar is mainly occupied "by carpenters and other objectionable traders" and should not be allowed to become an "eye-sore or a nuisance" to the European population in the vicinity. It suggested that it should be partially rebuilt after relieving congestion and after keeping provision for adequate light and air. It recommended that the evicted population could be accommodated in the buildings proposed to be constructed. Again, nothing practical was done and the bazar remains crowded and narrow, as it was then.

The 1907 Committee had also recommended the removal of the Kaithu Bazar but the 1914 Committee thought otherwise. It only suggested some improvements. Similarly it suggested certain improvements in the Ladakhi Mohalla, Boileauganj and Chhota Simla. The question of improvements in the Middle Bazar was left pending till a map of the area was completed. Most of the proposals, however, fell through. The Committee, realising the enormity of the task even at that stage concluded that "this will be the work of time, and can only be carried out by systematic operations carried out with some continuity of policy." It, however, remained only a dream.

An inter-linked, and equally important problem, was that of providing housing accommodation to the large number of Indian and European employees in the summer capital. A substantial number of employees had been added due to the shifting of the summer capital of Punjab and the Army Headquarters and the rents had soared up in proportion to the great demand for residential accommodation. The problem continues to remain serious till date despite vast expansion in the area of the town but while the Britishers were able to achieve better results through meticulous planning and execution of schemes, the plans never seem to take off in the modern day Simla.

Till just before the summer capital was shifted to Simla, most of the estates and residences in Simla were owned by British officers and non-officials. In the absence of government accommodation, these houses were rented annually for each 'season' to the government for housing offices and officers.

As the number of offices at Simla grew, the practice of renting out accommodation acquired the shape of a big lucrative business. It is on record that Major S.B. Goad was the owner of no less than thirty-three large estates in 1870s which had a rental value of about Rs. 38,000 per year. He was closely followed by Mr. J. Elston who owned thirty estates. Since the Simla Municipal Committee, in those days, was run according to a system in which the tax payers had a say in proportion to the tax they would pay, both Major Goad and Mr. Elston wielded great power.

Certain British officers, during their posting to Simla, also acquired estates. Their natural effort was to sell off the estate or the accommodation at the highest possible price before moving

out on transfer or retirement. They normally found rich and
extravagant buyers in the princes of Indian States who had also
begun to frequent Simla to be closer to the Imperial masters. Just
as in several major cities in India, the landlords prefer foreign
tenents who can pay higher rents, the landlords in Simla at that
time preferred to sell off the property to the obliging Rajas and
Ranas. The situation came to such a pass that some of them
acquired upto a dozen estates or houses in Simla. The time came
when the government began to feel alarmed after it was discover-
ed that about 20 per cent of all the good residential houses in the
town were owned by the Indian royal families. Though no official
orders were passed, the new transfer of properties in their name
was restricted. Among those declined permission to purchase a
house in Simla was the Nizam of Hyderabad who wanted to purchase the Snowdon building complex.

The British rulers also began discouraging the Indian princes
to stay put in Simla and in 1890 informal orders were issued asking the Indian princes not to "hang about" in Simla. They were
allowed to come on formal visits. Consequently, some of them
sold away their properties and only a negligible number retained
their estates in Simla.

That was by no means an end to the problem. Nor did the
fact that the number of houses in Simla rose from 290 in 1866 to
1,141 in 1881, prove much help to the increasing number of officials, both Indian and European. Efforts were then made to restrict the "unwanted" Indians, that is, those who were unemployed
and came to Simla to seek employment or those who had no business in the town. The Commissioner, Delhi Division, Mr. Fan-
shawe, in a letter to the Financial Secretary of the Punjab Government in 1899 wrote that Simla, "like a cantonment of our creation,
is the outcome of our rule and the peculiar conditions of that
rule, and there is no reason why we should admit persons to be
residents of the place except upon such conditions as we consider
necessary with regard to the peculiar conditions of it. Sentimental
reasons of freedom of movement and politico-economic reasons
of liberty of trade do not apply to such a case."

While the European officials were feeling the crunch, the situation of the much larger number of Indian clerks and officials was

even worse. A survey in 1914 revealed that the Indian clerk population in Simla was 1,435, with 2,056 dependents, and only 92 of
them were provided with government accommodation. The others
lived in rented and dingy houses in the various bazars. No less
than 652 clerks, exclusive of their dependents, lived in the Main
bazar area amidst most unhygienic conditions. It was felt that it
was important "both in the interests of the government and the
clerks" that more accommodation be built to house them. They
were actually the silent sufferers. Keeping in view the great shortage of accommodation, they were forced to pay exorbitant rents
and it was wisely decided that any increase in the house rent to
these employees would only benefit the landlords.

The Simla Improvement Committee noted in 1914 that the
government had mooted schemes in 1906 to construct enough
houses to accommodate at least two-thirds of the Indian employees
but "little has been done to attain this end, at any rate in the case
of the Indian clerks." The Committee suggested that the most suitable site for constructing government quarters would be between
the Phagli and the Dhar villages. The total area of the site was
about 90 acres. The Committee also proposed improvements in
the Nabha Estate, which contained a large number of small and
dingy buildings, where about 1000 porters resided in the limited
area of just five acres.

The 1917 report of the House Accommodation Committee
felt that "it is, however, generally recognised that some definite
policy in regard to accommodation is required, and that it is not
sufficient to wait untill the pressure becomes excessive and then to
meet it by the hurried acquisition or construction of additional
residences." The report strongly pleaded the case of the junior
European officers for whom the high rental charges "makes it
almost impossible" to find accommodation "within their means,
and it is highly undesirable in the interests of general efficiency,
that selected men should be prevented from taking up appointments at headquarters owing to their being unable to live in Simla
upon their pay."

The Committee confined itself mainly to the needs of the
Europeans on the plea that plans have already been drawn for the

Indian officials. The report suggested that the Punjab Government's Legislative Council should meet at Lahore rather than at Simla but felt that moving the Punjab Government's summer capital from Simla would not help much in relieving congestion and in providing any substantial increase in the availability of accommodation. It suggested several other measures, including some very harsh ones, to deal with the problem. Among other steps suggested by the Committee were the amendment to the relevant acts providing for the control of rents by the government and the reservation of houses for its employees, the imposition of tax on the sale and purchase of buildings and the acquisition of the right of pre-emption of property by the government to enable it to check speculation. Likewise it suggested that the question of imposing additional direct tax on non-officials could be considered and recommended that power should be taken to license all hotels in Simla and a condition for the licence being that accommodation should be placed at the disposal of government whenever required.

The population of the Indians, in the meantime, rose by leaps and bounds much to the chagrin of the planners. Some of the rich landlords and traders began purchasing posh houses solely on their capacity to pay the high price demanded by the Europeans who wanted to sell these houses before leaving Simla. The situation turned grave when no less than 38 good houses were purchased by Indians within a span of nine years from 1898. While the princes had taken the hint to vacate the place, the rich landlords and traders were not easily intimidated. In 1907 the Simla Improvement Committee report strongly recommended that no further big settlement, as the one at Nabha estate, should be allowed. It noted that the "prohibition against the acquisition of land by ruling chiefs in Simla should be rigorously enforced. In addition to Nabha settlement, there are at present, 29 houses in the Station Ward or European quarter which are occupied by natives" but it did not recommend the reservation of certain areas for Europeans. However, it noted that the question of reservation of areas for officials may have to be considered if the problem became acute.

Ultimately, the government decided to acquire 49 houses spread over an area of about a hundred acres in an effort to solve the problem of housing shortage in 1919. It also drew up fresh plans to tide over the shortage but the government was not really able to catch up with the fast growing population. Yet—to give due credit to the officers—they did make an earnest effort.

Simla witnessed a hectic building activity soon after the Imperial Government had firmly decided to retain it as the summer capital. The priority, obviously, was given to construct office buildings. The 'Gorton Castle', which housed the civil secretariat, and the Army Headquarters building were completed by 1885. These were closely followed by the buildings to accommodate the Public Works Department offices, the Foreign office, the Post and Telegraph office and the Government of India Press. Over Rs. 50 lakhs were spent on the construction of the various office buildings.

The most outstanding building constructed at that time, which has stood witness to a large number of historical events, was the Viceregal Lodge. Constructed at a cost of Rs. 16.5 lakh, the imposing building in the English Rennaissance style, was constructed by Henry Irwin, the local Superintendent of Works, and Captain H.H. Cole of the Royal Engineers. Although the Viceregal Lodge was occupied on July 23, 1888 by the then Viceroy Lord Dufferin, the work on its improvement was carried on for several years. 'Peterhoff', which remained the residence of successive Viceroys for 26 years, was considered too small for the purpose and in fact Lord Lytton had described it as "a sort of pigsty". Yet it was the house where "more illustrious heads rested at one time or other than in any other humble, five bedroom house in the Empire".

Lord Lytton sorely missed his privacy in the 'Peterhoff'. He wrote that he was not left alone even for a second: "I sit in the privatest corner of my private room and if I look through the window, there are two sentinels standing guard over me. If I go up and downstairs, an A.D.C. and three unpronounceable beings in white and red nightgowns with dark faces run after me. If I steal out of the house by the backdoor, I look around and find myself stealthily followed by a tail of fifteen persons."

He loved taste and style and had to make do with the small house. It is interesting to note the hospitality record of a single day, October 11, 1877, at the 'Peterhoff'. On that day alone there were 14 guests for lunch and 13 for dinner. They drank between themselves "six bottles of champagne, eight of claret, two of sherry, two of German beer, three of brandy and two of whiskey while their personal servants consumed another four bottles of claret, three of beer, four pints of porter and six glasses of brandy."

Lady Dufferin, in her *Our Vicergal Life in India* has described the house as a "cottage" which was suitable for "a domestic and not an official life—so, personally, we are comfortable; but when I look around my small drawing room and consider all the other diminutive apartments, I do feel that it very unfit for a Viceregal establishment." She has given a very amusing description of the house: "altogether it is the funniest place; at the back of the house you have about a yard to spare before you tumble down a precipice, and in front there is just room for one tennis court before you go over another." The 'Peterhoff', which was used as the High Court and Governor's House after the Independence, was totally destroyed in a major fire in 1981.

Lord Dufferin took an active interest in the construction of the Viceregal Lodge and himself suggested its general plan. In fact, one of his main occupations, as a means to relax from the official files, was to visit the site of construction and to discuss the building plans. His wife also often visited though she made the best use of 'Peterhoff' for the round of balls and parties. While on one of her visits to the building under construction she found "the work-people are really very amusing to look at, especially the young ladies in necklaces, bracelets, earrings, tight cotton trousers, turbans with long veils hanging down their backs, and a large earthenware basin of mortar on their heads. They walk about with the carriage of Empresses, and seem as much at ease on the top of the roof as on the ground-floor; most picturesque masons they are. The house will really be beautiful, and the views all round are magnificent." They occupied the new house on July 23, 1888.

It was during this period that Simla became the centre-stage of the Imperial Government. It was the focus of attention and a variety of important proclamations and orders were issued from time to time. However a decline in its importance commenced much before most people would have envisaged.

3
The Society
1861–1920

With the Raj at its acme of power and glory, it was not "all work and no play" at Simla. In fact, Simla attracted criticism for quite the contrary. It was the age of resplendent *memsahibs* and chivalrous *sahibs* served by an army of *khidmatgars*, *chupprasies*, *ayahs*, butlers, *coolies*, and others. It was an Anglo-Indian world of endless rounds of parties, balls, plays, fancy dress functions, dances and games which a writer in the satirical journal *Vanity Fair* once summed up as "duty and red tape, picnics and adultery." The lavish life-style also brought into stark contrast the pathetic conditions of the "natives" the difference between the ruler and the ruled notwithstanding. The particular circumstances at Simla only heightened the irony and some European visitors to Simla during that period also did not fail to note it.

The prevailing "tone of Simla society", as Andrew Wilson stated, was set by the Viceroy and his wife. Both Lord Mayo and Lord Northbrook set a tone of "worthy diligence and earnest endeavour that did not add much colour and gaiety" to the town but things began hotting up after Lord Lytton's arrival. He and his wife took immense interest in the town and the society. Almost every evening, the 'Peterhoff' was the venue of balls and fancy dress parades. He also took great interest in theatre and it was during his tenure that the theatre movement received a fillip in Simla. Theatre became a symbol of "intellectual amusement" and many Europeans patronised it just for the sake of pretensions and prestige but there were some genuine lovers of theatre too.

Though the first mention of theatre in Simla dates back to 1838 when Emily Eden wrote about the staging of some plays, it was the effort of Lord Lytton which made Simla the "Mecca of amateur actors". Lord Lytton himself produced his self-written play in 1878 called "Walpole". He also acted as its director, stage manager and is said to have spent several days in preparing to stage the play. Even his wife is stated to have acted in two plays staged at 'Peterhoff'.

He was mainly instrumental in the construction of a regular new theatre, the Gaiety theatre, which stands till date. The old theatre also continued to remain in use till the big fire in May 1889 completely gutted it. The Gaiety theatre opened in 1887 with the play "Time will Tell". The Amateur Dramatic Club (A.D.C.) was handed over the possession of the theatre in the following year. In those days the theatre used to earn something like Rs. 9,500 to Rs. 11,000 from the boxes alone on the first and second nights of each new play. It used to produce some of the best London plays and was a fore-runner for amateur theatre in the country. Almost every week a new play was staged and a record number of 29 plays were staged during 1896 with some of them running for upto eleven nights at a stretch. Till that year the theatre continued to be lighted by oil lamps and the introduction of electricity made it all the more attractive.

The theatre also passed through some difficult times but there were enough theatre-enthusiasts who voluntarily came out to help it tide over the difficulties during that period. The theatre saw a sharp decline after the Britishers left Simla, so much so that no play was staged in the theatre between 1954 and 1964 and only one play was staged in the next decade. Though the A.D.C. still exists, the club has been rented to the army authorities and plays are sometimes staged but these are rare and far between. It is now mainly used for official functions and cultural activities and seminars. It was the theatre with which great men like Rudyard Kipling and Van Prinsep, and in our times Prithvi Raj Kapoor and Kundan Lal Sehgal, remained associated. In fact, Sehgal began his career here as a musician before he made a mark as a great singer.

Another chief source of attraction for the European society in those days, besides the theatre for "intellectual amusements", was the Annandale ground where picnics, fetes and fancy dress shows were regularly held. The game of croquet was one of the favourites of the Europeans. It became a popular haunt during the reign of Lord Lytton.

His successor Lord Ripon was not as social as Lord Lytton was but Lord Dufferin, who came in next, left no one in doubt when he declared that he preferred "men and women to trees" and together with his wife injected new enthusiasm in the European society. They took active interest in the social life. Major General Nigel Woodyatt has in his *Under Ten Viceroys* described an incident at a fancy dress ball given by the Dufferins at the Viceregal Lodge. He has written that he was dancing with a beautiful lady when an Arab appeared and began talking to the lady. He wrote that he felt quite irritated and told the lady: "oh; come along, never mind that old Arab. He is thinking of 'Lillie Langtry', his donkey at Port Said". The lady did not budge, though still holding his arm, but looked quite embarrassed. "I looked more closely at the intruder and recognised Lord Dufferin."

He has described Lord Dufferin as "a great ladies man" and has related another anecdote thus: "Assembling his personal staff soon after his arrival in India, Lord Dufferin explained his wishes regarding ceremonial functions and the attention necessary to all guests at Government House." "I want you to quite understand" he said, "that I expect you to devote your energies to the elderly ladies. You need not trouble about the young and pretty ones, I will look after them myself."

Several interesting accounts of the European society in Simla as it was then, have been left by the residents and visitors to the town. Iris Portal, who was born in Simla, and later returned as a teenager, wrote, "In the two summers that I spent at Simla I never thought about doing anything but amusing myself. It was excessively gay. My record was twenty-six nights dancing, at the end of which I would hardly keep awake, but I had to attend an official dinner that my mother was giving and was severely reprimanded for falling asleep in the middle when talking to a very woolly old judge." She further wrote that she was always "meeting the same people, everyone knew rather too much about everyone else's affairs, and it was a staple topic of conversation what was going on, who was going out with so-and-so. If there was a very big party you always knew about it and if you had'nt been invited you took that very seriously."

Ian Stephens wrote that "it was a whirl of entertainment, inter-spread with some quite gorgeous ceremonial and pomp, parti-cularly, in the Viceroy's house."

Sir Henry Sharp wrote in *Good-bye India* that Simla's greatest "asset was the gay and gifted society that collected. If you wanted fun, there were plenty of young and cherry souls." Many dashing youngmen thronged Simla either for better prospects or just for amusement. As Carey, a local architect put it in 1870, "the utter absence of occupation on the one hand, and on the other, the keen search after amusement, let it be what it may, makes life go at a reckless hard gallop that many come out of in a sore plight."

Where youth and beauty met, romance was inevitable, goes the popular saying. It consequently gave rise to flirtations and petty jealousies. Those who went after the ladies were known as "poodle-fakers" and were said to come down from the hill, "fighting rear-guard action against the husbands coming up." Both the circumstances and surroundings were highly conducive for romance. Iris Portal wrote "it is difficult to say how enor-mously romantic the atmosphere was in Simla, the warm scarlet nights and bright huge moon, those towering hills and mountains stretching away silence and strange exotic smells. Very often coming home from dance the current boy friend used to walk by the side of the rickshaw, murmuring sweet notings and holding hands over the side of the hood, nothing much more than that, but it was very romantic. Everything was intensely romantic—and a lot of people were lonely."

A write-up that appeared in the *Pioneer* said that "nowhere possibly in the world are the passions of human nature laid so open for dissection as they are on the remote hill stations on the slopes of the eternal abodes of snow. In the very small commu-nities the round of gossip is incessant, probably inevitable. Re-sources there are none save such as are afforded by amusement committees. The men are mostly deprived of sport, the women are over-laden with calls and dressing and admiration."

It had then, as it has now, the small-town mentality. Gossip and scandalising was the order of the day. False social values and artificiality thrived. A system of "calling", which was introduced several decades ago when the European population was very small, developed into a farce. Under the "calling" system each new-comer to the town was supposed to call on at the residences of others. With the growth of population, it became almost impossible to call on at all the European residents. A system was evolved to ease the problem and simply visiting cards were placed in the letter boxes to indicate the identity of the "caller". Later, groups of new-comers decided to divide the labour and form "leagues" which went in different directions to put the cards in letter boxes. Several amusing incidents of such a practice are related. One is about a young man who visited Simla just for amusement and spent most of his time in playing golf. He asked some friends to distribute his cards. One evening he attended a dance and apologised to a lady next to him for not being able to call on her. The lady curtly replied that on the contrary judging by the number of cards he had left at her house, he had called on her no less than thirty-two times!

The European society of those days also came in for sharp criticism from some of the writers and visitors. Val Princep wrote that "real sociability does not exist . . . people pair off directly they arrive at a party as a matter of course, and the pairs, happy in their own conversation, do not trouble themselves about the general hilarity." The society was structured solely on civil service and military hierarchies, and since he was merely an artist, he was frequently "left out in the cold." *The Times* Correspondent W.H. Russell had noted as early as 1858 that the social distinctions are perhaps more rigidly observed at Simla than those back home. He wrote that, "each man depends on his position in the public service, which is the aristocracy; and those who do not belong to it are out of the pail, no matter how wealthy they may be, or what claims they may advance to the consideration of the world around them. The women depend on the rank of their husbands. Mrs. A the wife of a barrister making $ 4,000 or 5,000 a year, is nobody as compared with Mrs. B whose husband is a Deputy Commissioner or Mrs. C who is the better half of the Station Surgeon. Wealth can do nothing for man or woman in securing them honour or precedence in their march to dinner, or on their way to supper table, or in a dance." This, Princep, realised in 1877 and did not regret leaving Simla while writing sarcastically; "at length I have left Simla with its civilised gaieties and scandals, and can resume my journal with some chance of recording something more than the flirtation of Capt. A with Mrs. B, or the quarrels and jealousies of C and his wife, which form the staple conversation of the modern Capua swelled by the tittle-tattle of the Viceroy . . ."

Yet another side of the picture has been provided by Mrs. Walter Tibbids in *The Voice of the Orient,* while on a visit to Simla during 1909: "There are many worlds in Simla. The noisiest is that circle of men and women who have no higher ideal in life than to win a prize in a "bumble puppy", to be seen speaking to a Vicerine or to have an A.D.C. as an attache . . . the tongue is the most potent weapon known in Simla. It is indeed mightier than the sword, and the fear of the society grips the firmest foundation of morals. Men who would step unflinchingly up to the cannon's mouth walk warily before the eagle eyes of the Simla dowagers."

The worst criticism, however, came from Rudyard Kipling who mocked at the society through his verses and other writings. Particularly interesting is his poem "Gleesome Fleasome Thou" in which he hits severely at the society through verses in praise of *bunders* (monkeys):

"Artful *bunder*, who, never in his life,
had flirted at Peliti's with another *bunder's* wife"

The Peliti's was one of the favourite hotels frequented by Europeans, particularly married women and young men. He also lampooned the society in Simla in his *Plain Tales from the Hills* and his character Mrs. Hawksbees symbolised the young women at Simla. Several residents of Simla, however, retorted that he had highly exaggerated his description and characters.

The European society in Simla was also widely criticised in various newspapers, and Edward J. Buck believes that newsmen had little else to report so they and "jaundiced critics" gave detailed and often exaggerated account of fun and frivolities in Simla. Those who were opposed to the shifting of the summer capital from Calcutta to Simla found the reports a handle to beat the Government with.

Both the English and the vernacular press frequently published reports and letters denouncing the society which was a "blot on the fair name" of England and renewed appeals were made to bring back the summer capital to Calcutta. The officials who were left behind in Calcutta while their "privileged" colleagues went to the cool climate of Simla, obviously resented the move. The press, which thrived in Calcutta due to easy availability of sources and which had to wait for news to trickle down after several days from Simla, did not relish the absence of the government machinery from Calcutta for long duration every year. The traders, who made fortunes when the secretariat was permanently stationed in Calcutta also felt the crunch when it remained absent for nearly eight months every year.

The reasons advanced by them in favour of retaining the capital at Calcutta included a poor transportation and communication system connecting Simla. Indeed, the transportation system was quite bad till improvements were made in the road linking Kalka with Simla towards the end of the 19th century and the railway between the two places was commissioned in the early years of the 20th century. Till then hardly a year passed when the traffic was not disrupted for a few days every year due to landslides which resulted in the summer capital remaining cut-off from the rest of the country during that period.

The most severe criticism and ridicule was, however, reserved for fairs, picnics, balls, dances and "other frivolities" in which the government officials, were charged with indulging in during their "jaunt" to Simla.

The newspapers were almost inundated with reports of merry-making and "wastage of time" at Simla. A substantial number of letters from readers were also in the same vein. I would here like to quote a part of a letter written to the editor of the *Statesman* by a "sojourner" who called himself 'Cantab'. He wrote: "Sir— will you allow me to use a phrase less elegant than expressive and to say that many of us Simla sojourners are thoroughly 'fed up' with its unmitigated frivolities week in, week out. I agree that occasional fun and play are also (essential) and send a worker back to work, with renewed zest, but when, as in Simla, play is the rule and not the exception; when day after day shows but a long programme of vanities and inanities, picnics, fetes, 'some lucky bags', and gymkhanas, followed by dances at night—when this is the perpetual pabulam offered to grown up British men and women, is it any wonder if some get satiated with the fare".

"Even in Simla there are some who take work seriously, though the environing atmosphere certainly discourages that view. There are still those who believe that the Government of India is an institution founded and paid for the one object of administering the country in an earnest spirit. In order to carry out its trust efficiently was not the 'Calcutta exodus' started on the one side and the Simla exodus on the other, so that the relaxing climate of the commercial capital in the summer and autumn might be avoided, and the too bracing climate of Simla in the winter shunned, all for the one purpose of letting our legislators work for the better? There is no other excuse of the anomaly of the two capitals in India; with the consequent enormous expense to the country than that put forward on the plea of work".

"We do not ask whether the Government of India might not survive the Calcutta climate equally with those who carry on there, their strenuous work throughout the year. What we do ask is whether the deliberate waste of time which is the 'the correct thing' in Simla is not a scandal and a blemish on British rule? For instance, Sir, are you aware that the Government of India is actually held up for two days in order that Simla may attend the 'Sipi' fair? For not one but two days the wheels of the government, the law courts, the treasury, etc. cease to go round in order that Simla amuse itself at native fair. That one instance gives the key-note to the music of the Simla season. Is there a single month in the year in which there are not several holidays? and the few days that are not public holidays are not almost sure to be broken up by some tennis contest or fete of some sort. If two-thirds of the year must be spent here, what work is being got through. Is Simla the playground of India? Meantime, in the name of the momentous responsibilities to which the British have been called in India, and have accepted, let us retrieve our reputation. Let us cease to make Simla the Popinjay among the capitals of the Empire".

But there were also those who were in favour of retaining Simla as the summer capital and the reply to 'Cantab's' letter was equally interesting. It was written by one 'Almis' and published on July 11, 1913 in the *Statesman*. "Sir, one is doubtful whether Cantab's letter in your issue of the 8th is meant to be taken seriously or not. He complains that he is 'fed up' with Simla's unmitigated frivolities. Is he, then, compelled to take part in them? Will he lose his billet (assuming he has one up there) if he does not attend 70 per cent of the dances and 81.3 per cent of gymkhanas? Are there no holidays in busy strenuous Calcutta? Are not the law courts, the secretariat and the treasuries etc. in Calcutta 'held up', as Cantab puts it annually, not for two days but for a fortnight at a stretch during the Pujas and do not the Calcutta law courts have an even longer vacation at another period of the year? Even in hustling England, are bank holidays and King's birthdays and Empire days quite unknown? Do not places of business close for Christmas holidays? Are no government offices 'held up' for two or three days at a stretch at Easter? Does Calcutta has no dances, no theatres, no races, no belvedere fetes, no picnics, no crickets, no tennis, 'no vanities and inanities' ".

"And at home do none of our over-worked statesmen and ministers indulge in a round of dinners and lunches and dances and receptions; do none of them look in at operas and theatres, horse-races, flower-shows, olympias, aviation meets and the like. If the above things are indulged in money-making Calcutta and roaring, hustling England, why single out Simla as a 'Popinjay among capitals' "?

"When Cantab writes of government being held up for two days does he quite understand what he is writing about? Does he know that the business of government never ceases? That even if a certain day is declared a holiday, there are men on duty in every office to attend urgent matters? That the more important offices have arrangements for receiving pressing work at every, at any hour of the night, let alone during the day time? Let every official, no matter how high in the scale he may be, is liable to be called away from his amusements or roused from his slumbers at all hours of the day and night to attend to matters of urgency".

"Cantab, I suspect, does not belong to official circles. He probably sees a superficial butterfly existence of the Capital but has not been behind the scenes. He has seen an official rush away from office at 3 P.M. to attend a gymkhana, but has not seen that same official, on his return home, buried under office boxes, which keep him busy till dinner time. Nor has he seen him after dinner (when the world supposes him to be amusing himself) burning the mid-night oil, mastering complicated cases, setting in order the chaos he had received from local governments. Cantab will doubtless be surprised to hear of officials who, after a dance, are contended with three or four hours' sleep, settle to work early in the morning, attend office at the prescribed hour, put in a hard day's work there and leave off work just in time to dress for dinner. In support of his charge that government has 'lost touch' and the like, what concrete case can Cantab put forward? In my humble opinion, nothing short of a Royal commission can prove or disprove accusations of this nature".

"The above, Sir, is life in Simla in a nutshell, and strenuous work and strenuous play, how strenuous both are of their kind, the listless and parboiled dweller on the gangetic triangle can scarcely realise".

Though the particular letter writer and some others, who shared his views, tried to justify the existence of Simla as the summer capital they were largely out-numbered by those who were highly critical of it. Shortly after the above-noted letter was published in the *Statesman*, the newspaper office received a horde of letters. I will quote the one by 'Glasweg'. It said, "Sir, I gather from the letter of Almis that if the hardworked secretaries to the government and the other officials at Simla ever do snatch an hour or two during the day in order to take part in a gymkhana they make it up for it by 'slogging' before dinner and late into the night in order to evolve order out of the 'chaos' which they have received from local government. It is the very pretty picture which, if accepted in its entirety, would almost appear to justify the generous manner in which titles and decorations are sprinkled about among headquarters officials on every possible occasion. Unfortunately the public knows too much to believe in any such picture" and he went on to relate an incident which happened in Delhi (which he frankly admitted) and not in Simla.

He wrote that a story was circulating about a non-official member associated with an official meeting. The work could not be completed till the lunch time. He suggested to the official members that they could again meet after lunch. The official members said that they would be busy in "still more important" work. Therefore, it was decided that the meeting be adjourned till the next morning. The non-official member who had no engagements in the afternoon decided to go and watch a polo match to while away his time. There to his dismay he found those very officials busy in the "still more important work" of watching the polo!

The letter narrated another story about an under-secretary who used to remain absent from his office quite frequently. When his peon was asked whether the under-secretary was ill, he replied in the negative and said that his master remained in his house to practice violin for some concert at the government house or elsewhere. Yet another story going the rounds was about a government official who delayed an important decision for two or three years. It was said that at Calcutta he would tell his staff to bring the files before him at Simla and at Simla he would ask them to bring the files at Calcutta!

The president of the European Defence Association, Mr. Dudley Myers once visited Simla and wrote quite flatteringly about it. The reaction was strong and immediate. A member of his own association wrote: "I must confess that I am profoundly disappointed with Mr. Myers, and I question whether on this subject his views are not in total disagreement with those of the body over which he presides." Another letter held the views of Mr. Myers as "amusing" and yet another said that, "I have no doubt that the 'popinjay capital' will be much obliged to Mr. Myers for his testimonial, but to my mind it is not very satisfactory to find the president of the European Defence Association defending a system which is condemned by 99 out of every 100 non-official Europeans in India, because it is contrary to their interests."

A letter to *The Times* in 1917 stated that "if the people of England desire to see any real report of our system of government in India they will insist upon a Parliamentary enquiry into the abuse which has gradually grown up within the last half century of conducting the administration for seven months of the year from the distant hill station of India. The station is so remote that the influence of what little public opinion is there in India is hardly felt by the government during its long annual seclusion there, while the extent of the demoralisation of the public services which results from its annual migration to what is in many respects a mere pleasure resort is still suspected in this country."

It went on to say that Simla is a regular retreat of a host of avowed pleasure-seekers who go there on leave, and, having no work to occupy them, pass their time in a long round of frivolity and gaiety, in which the idle and the unemployed expect that those who are there on duty shall be as much at leisure as themselves. In ordinary times the station is full of idle military men and civilians, dangling attendance upon the wives and daughters of men absent in the plains, and amusement is main object and pursuit of all. Articles frequently appeared under such headlines as "Revels on Olympus". Few believed those who attempted to defend the European society at Simla. Despite Lord Curzon's assertion that "Simla is no longer a holiday resort of an epicurean Viceroy and a pampered government." The revellers were, in fact, hardly bothered about the Viceroy and the government.

And while the European society in Simla was enjoying the best of times, the plight of the 'natives' was pathetic. Though the treatment meted out to the Indians was never good, the peculiar circumstances of the two groups at Simla during that period sharpened the irony. As talking about the plight of the rickshaw pullers in 1834, A.G. Clow pointed out that the plight of the rickshaw pullers "is frequently heightened by the contrast between the circumstances of the passenger and of those conveying him, possibly to an evening's diversion or hospitality. The truism that the men would not come if they did not secure a financial benefit by so doing is not a complete answer to such doubts." For instance, Lady Wilson, in her *Letters from India* gave a description of the life in Simla while contrasting the two classes: "I hear nothing but rickshaws whirling past, their bells tinkling and their runners shouting 'take care' to the rickshawmen in front, all of them, according to my imagination, carrying over-wrought humanity to their 23rd or possibily 40th consecutive *tamasha*, a ball, a play, a concert or more probably the inevitable *bara khana*."

The early writers and visitors to Simla have left very few references about the Indian society. Obviously all the references are from the European point of view and, unfortunately, no account by any Indian is available. However, the writings of the European visitors give an insight to the conditions of the 'natives' and one can draw inferences. Like a French traveller, M. Victor Jacquemont, who visited the area in 1831, made passing reference to the leash under which the Indians were kept by the British rulers. He wrote: "it is rather difficult to procure porters for luggage ... but Captain Kennedy has obligingly offered to imprison any of mine who refuse to accompany me . . . ."

Captain Mundy, in his *Journal of a Tour in India* has given an instance of how "erring" Indians were made to learn a lesson in 1828 which could deter even the bravest among them. For the mere act of beating a British officer, who had allegedly humiliated them, two Indian sepoys were ordered to be given 800 lashes each in full view of the public. That was not all and they were both dismissed from service "without any loss of time."

One of the most arduous task of the Indians, particularly during the early days, was to carry heavy loads from the plains in the absence of roads. The "groaning coolies", who carted the bag and baggage of *mai baps* and *mem sahibs*, were mainly *begar* labour. Since there was a great shortage of porters, people were picked up from the villages and fields and forced to carry the luggage. Emily Eden's diary, *Up the Country* gives a clue to the number of porters required even as early as 1838 for the Viceroy's entourage. She wrote that "every camel trunk takes an average of eight men, and we have several hundred camel trunks of stores alone, Colonel T., the Political Agent, had, however, arrived with a reinforcement of coolies and everything was progressing."

There were, of course, people whose conscience pricked them but there was little else they could do. Ian Stephens wrote that "the annual move to Simla was romantic, but rather horrifying. The memory that sticks in my mind is of those coolies pulling and humping terribly heavy loads on their backs up hill slopes. I felt the same repungence to travelling around Simla in a rickshaw. Eventually, I got accustomed to it but never quite used to it." Many of the porters fell ill at Simla and particularly those coming from Calcutta could not adjust themselves to the hill conditions and faced the problem of acclimatisation. They dreaded visiting Simla, and, as Emily Eden wrote, "I suppose this is a very bad Siberia to them."

She wrote in her diary that "all the native servants are, or have been sick, and I do not wonder. We have built 20 small houses since we came, and have lodged 50 of our servants in these outhouses, still, there were always a great many looking unhappy, so I made J. to go round to all the houses and get me a list of all who were settled, and of those whose houses were not built, and I found there were actually 67 who had no lodging provided for them. I should like to hear the row English servants would have made, and these are not a bit more used to rough it. There is not one who has not his own little house at Calcutta, and his wife to cook for him; so they feel the cold and their helplessness doubly, but they never complain . . . as these men have only four shillings a week for themselves and families, of course they can save nothing, and if they are turned away at a distance from home they really may die of starvation."

The Indians were treated with contempt, and their customs and traditions were mocked at, and related with a condescending manner. While most Europeans resisted a temptation for beef and cared for the religious sentiments of the locals, there were some who did not bother for the restrictions by local chieftains when they had initially begun to settle in the area.

In his book, Charles French noted that the slaughter of cow was prohibited on account of the "prejudices of the natives" but "now this rule is somewhat more honoured in its breach than in its observance." The Rajas and Ranas were initially recognised and as the decades advanced they were merely seen as persons who brought them caravans laden with rich gifts. A certain amount of contempt for their effort to mix up with the Europeans was evident. During the later part of the 19th century, their sojourns to Simla and efforts to purchase property prompted the government to hint them that they should not "hang about" in Simla—and most of them obligingly withdrew.

An amusing instance is related about a Maharaja, who while watching a play, heard the following verse:

"When my wife against my will
Goes out, I never stops her;
But when she's gone a little way
I calls her back and 'whops' her".

Val Prinsep, who has mentioned the episode, wrote that at the Maharaja's request, the Foreign Secretary translated the verse in as best manner as he could. The Maharaja, he wrote, turned grave and said: "We do not do that, we should'nt let our wives go out at all." Prinsep added that perhaps the Maharaja mistook the verse with an English man's behaviour and had thought that "Lord Lytton continually whops his lady." But returning back to the common 'natives', they continued to be used as *jhampanees* and hand-rickshaw-pullers who carried the *mem sahibs* to their rounds of "callings", parties and fetes.

During the first war of Indian Indpendence, the Indian residents of Simla proved to be quite "harmless and docile" but it helped in changing the outlook of only a few European residents. There were others who sought to seek revenge on them for the "excesses" committed by some of their countrymen in other parts of the Empire. The local authorities, however, expressed gratitude and advised tolerance towards the Indian residents.

The "Mutiny Record Reports" state the story of one Rampershad of Sabathu near Simla who was suddenly arrested on the charge of being the writer of some seditious letters and who was taken to Ambala where he was summarily executed. The reports mentioned that the letters were unquestionably seditious but hold that Rampershad seem to "have been a victim of conspiracy". It was learnt that he was in fact an illiterate and could not have possibly written the letters which, interestingly, were found from the regular mailman which was known to be checked quite thoroughly during those days. The Deputy Commissioner in his report pointed out that Rampershad possessed considerable wealth and had made himself "obnoxious" to one creditor at least by the enforcement of somewhat stringent measures for the recovery of his claims. The tragedy apart, the Deputy Commissioner at least had the moral courage to admit the lapse.

Referring to the rather docile behaviour of the Indian residents of Simla, Lt. Mawwell's report said that, "whatever may have been the real sentiments, all classes of the natives, who were under my observation, at all times, evinced the best possible feelings towards ourselves individually and towards our cause. I always did and do now utterly disbelieve in the supposed readiness of the native servants and others to rise and massacre the residents. I never did share these apprehensions, and I invariably found that they were entertained chiefly by those most ignorant of the people. So far from harbouring such suspicions of the natives here, I always thought and always shall think that in adhering to our cause and refraining from injuring us in our helpless hour they afforded the best practical proof of their utter want of sympathy in this military rebellion." Referring to the attitude towards the Indians, he wrote that, "I cannot understand that sort of discrimination which sees no difference between the guilty and the innocent, and which, because certain natives have behaved ill at Cawnpore, would punish certain others who behaved well at Kussolie."

In his report the Deputy Commissioner wrote that the "conduct of the native servants appears to me to have been creditable to them, and I cannot at this moment recall a single well-authenticated case of insolence or improper behaviour towards any European in any way traceable to the mutiny or affording any proof of the offender being actuated by motives inimical to the British. To judge by the language generally held, our countrymen had lost all notion of justice. Expression was given to this feeling by a loud cry for the extension of Martial Law to Simla, not because guilty men had been allowed to escape, but simply because Martial Law was supposed to afford greater facilities for taking revenge on men whose only crime was their dark skin . . . ."

His other mention in the report also reflects the change in the attitude of some British officers towards the Indians. He wrote that "the truth is, one has now to guard against, not a tendency to be lenient to natives, but the very contrary feeling, and I am sure most officers will admit that in every case in which a native is on one side and a European on the other, it is most difficult to avoid a bias in favour of the latter."

To the great majority of the European residents of Simla, the Indians were mainly "red-leveried" *Chuprassies*, the most conspicous symbol of the British Raj and "thoroughly bad servants." The *Chuprassies* were ubiquitous and performed a variety of service. As Deborah Morris, in *With Scarlet Majors*, described them as persons who "met trains, squatted outside offices, despatched telegrams and opened doors, carried files and cups of tea, and in their almost unlimited spare time, spun hunks of crude cotton yarn and knitted it up with pull-overs." They were actually considered by the Indians as quite powerful and influential. However, their worst condemnation has come from Aberigh-Mackay who described them as "mother-in-law of liars, the high priest of extortioners and receiver-general of bribes."

Edward J. Buck was "unable to find in any old or indeed in any new record of Simla a single complimentary remark on the native servants of the station" till 1925 and noted that nearly every writer of early years has advised that servants should be brought from the plains. But he also stated that some Simla residents believed that the local servants were "spoilt" by those coming from the plains. He quoted Andrew Wilson as writing that "Simla is famous for its bad servants." They were thought to be mean and cunning and out to fleece the Europeans.

A write-up in the Indian Planters' gazette in 1885 about Indian servants described them as "vasty deeps" of duplicity who had the "incompetence and general 'cussedness' of the Aryan domestic. Dirty, plausible, extravagant, useless, provoking, ill-competent, and, in short, unspeakable." It suggested that the government should do "something to help helpless Europeans towards securing a passable supply of fairly honest and capable domestics."

In his *Four Months Camping in the Himalayas,* Dr.W.G.N. Van Der Sleen, relates how he came to Simla to start an expedition and needed servants to carry his baggage. He writes, " . . . . and you don't have to look out for them. They come to you. For instance every European whose arrival is announced in the Simla Papers finds a row of silent figures squatting outside his bedroom door in the morning. They rise and *salaam* as you appear and with a murmur of *salaam sahib* thrust into your hands a big bundle of letter in which they are described as willing and capable to do anything and everything, and more besides. There is no difficulty in sifting out the first batch, as you instantly dismiss all who are unable to reply in English to an English question. As these generally represent about three-fourths of the applicants one may conclude that education here is not on an exceptionally high level. Then you deal with those that remain. When you discover that a single remark on your part about a dirty shirt or grubby hands is sufficient to relieve you, not only of the case in question, but of several other candidates for your favour as well."

"At last only five are left, three of whom have credentials, apparently bought or borrowed, in half a dozen different names. Which brings us to number four. This is a pugnacious-looking Mohammaden with a heavy beard. He looks down demurely scarce venturing to meet my gaze, but when I dismiss him there is a treacherous glitter in his eyes. I did it to test him. This reduces us to one man. He describes himself as a Christian, speaking timidly and folding his hands in the usual submissive Hindu fashion. But while I am looking at his papers his eyes keep wandering about the room, weighing up and measuring every item of our luggage. And when my wife happens to let some money chink in her hand, he gives one quick glance, in her direction and drops his eyes again. A humbug with a spurious character, so out with him too! This makes a clean sweep. But no sooner do we come in from our walk then there is another set of waiting figures. And after lunch yet another, two of whom we order to come back later. And so on and at the intervals throughout the day, they post themselves outside the door and there they stand, ready with their *salaam sahib* whenever you come out."

Though fed with reports to remain careful of the Indian servants, Dr. Sleen was candid in his admission after his tour that "it is impossible to get any insight into the life of the people. The distinction between European and native being too great to allow of any intercourse. For this, one had better to go to Bombay or Delhi or even Madras, where the educated native is in many respects the social equal of Europeans." The same feeling was expressed by Aberigh-Mackay when he wrote that "at a bureaucratic Simla dinner party, the abysses of ignorance that yawns below the company on every Indian topic was appalling."

At the opening of the Simla Fine Arts Society's exhibition in 1880, the Society's president boasted that all the greatest artists were from Europe but "there are a vast number of useful objects which native artisans can not only be brought to manufacture excellently well, but on which applications of resources of native indigenous ornaments are both agreeable and suitable." They seemed confident of the "superiority" of their civilisation and culture as compared to the ancient culture and art of India or were they simply displaying the instinct of self-preservation?

Edwin Montagu, who visited India in 1918 wrote on his arrival at Simla: "down-hill on a rickshaw is on the first experience terrifying, and uphill is at best miserable. One's feeling for the unfortunate men, who seem to be struggling, as their breath comes more laboured, is indescribable. In England, even in a four-in-hand, one would get out and walk up some of these steep hills. Nobody, even the most humane, seems to do it in India. I shall definitely set myself not to rebel against the order as I find it, and to express no opinion; so I merely conclude that long training and practice make it an easy for these men to pull a rickshaw, let us say, as an English agricultural labour were to work all day at a harvest. And I did notice that, coming home, when I imagined the men would be most tired the passing of another rickshaw produced a spontaneous and enthusiastic burst which could not be accounted for except on the theory which all the inhabitants seem to hold."

"But I am told by Dane (Lieutenant Governor of Punjab at that time) that rickshaw men all die early of lung disease."

He also mentioned about Lord Nickleson, the then Chairman on the Commission on Military Expenditure in India, who advised him at a dinner in Simla, "never to talk to my servants as this was harmful to prestige. Again I make no comments." He further wrote that, "I am again struck with the patriotism and devotion to efficiency of the Indian civilians and soldiers, but must suspend judgement on the equally striking superficial aloofness and apparent lack of interest in the Indian citizens of the country." He wrote feelingly about the poor masses and felt that the Europeans should not be so extravagant. He warned that, "there may be trouble and an unpopular Viceroyalty and bitterness but it should be done. I think I could do it. If I felt weak, I would give the money I saved to charity. It would help to stop the growth of luxury which Indian agitation is carefully watching. People should lead simple working life at Simla and it should be like a cabinet minister's weekend rather than a summer resort."

Conditions regulating society in Simla changed slightly during the 1920s with the emergence of "brown sahibs". The European society became more tolerant towards them as Buck noted in 1925: "moreover the fact that Indian ladies and gentlemen are now joining freely with their European friends in social entertainments has made a sensible difference. This fact has perhaps been inevitable with the appointment of Indian gentlemen who hold high official positions, but there are certain Indian ladies and gentlemen whose social qualities and generous hospitality have had a marked effect in this direction."

But Buck's assertion that the Indian men and women were "joining freely" in social functions with the Europeans was certainly exaggerated. The social contact, at best, was only at a superficial level. The Maharajas or wealthy chiefs of some States and Indian officials at very senior rungs of officialdom did, of course, had to attend the social functions but most Europeans eyed them with contempt. To quote a Simla resident Dr. B.R. Nanda, who was born in Simla during 1917 and has stayed in the town since then, the "difference in social attitude stood in the way" of good relations between the Indians and the Europeans. He relates that even the Indian gentry, including those belonging to royal families, would not eat at the parties fearing that beef was cooked or they were actually invited to join "after lunch or after dinner." Even the wealthy Maharajas, who used to stay at the Cecil hotel, preferred to get their food from vegetarian hotels run by Indians. The Indians, he asserts, were also not keen on mixing with the British because "which Indian women would have danced with them" and the social gatherings were nothing but a "round of drinks." He recalls that he had not seen the face of any Indian women even in the Lower Bazar, what to talk of the parties. The women used to be invariably in *ghunghat* or *burqua*. He asserts that common Indians had "no identity" and the British "kept a distance and there was no change in their attitude till the very last."

As late as in 1937, Sir Edmund Blunt, in order to attract Englishmen to join the Indian Civil Service, wrote about the army of servants they would require: "He will have to provide himself with a bearer, who looks after his clothes and rules his household, and (if his bearer is a Hindu) also a Mohammedan table servant (*Khidmatgar*), for no Hindu will wait at his table except to serve drinks; a *dhobi* to wash his clothes, and a sweeper (who emptied and cleaned the latrines or where these existed, looked after the lavatories). When he sets up a house of his own, he will need more servants; a cook and possibly a *bhisti*, who fetches water; also a garden staff, consisting of a gardener (*mali*) and a coolie or two. If he is living in a place where electricity is not available, he will also require transport and horse involving two more servants, a groom and a grass-cutter. . . . "

A member of British Parliament Mr. Robert Wallace, writing in the *Contemporary Review* expressed his fear of the "detrimental influence on English life of those who returned after exercising despotism over conquered peoples," and he described the behaviour of an average Anglo-Indian as "offensive to any man of democratic spirit." Labour was almost dust-free because the payment was entirely at the discretion of the Europeans. No one dared raise a voice. The rickshaw-pullers, for instance, were paid just eight annas if the rickshaw was engaged upto 12 hours and one rupee if it was engaged for 12 to 24 hours in Simla during 1900. The men were paid two annas each if they were engaged upto two hours, four annas each if they were engaged for 12 hours and eight annas each if their services were required for a period upto 24 hours. But not all Europeans paid according to the fixed rates.

A.G. Clow supervised an enquiry into the economic conditions of Simla rickshaw-pullers which was conducted in great detail by I.R. Dawar in 1934. The survey revealed that there were 450 rickshaws registered with the Municipal Committee in 1926. The number of rickshaws registered increased to 517 in 1932 but showed a slight decline in the following year when their number stood at 478. That year 2,707 men were registered with the Committee as rickshaw-pullers. Since Simla had no local labour, the rickshaw-pullers used to come each summer from the neighbouring areas and also places as far as Jullunder. The rates were fixed by the Committee and in 1934, the rate per rickshaw and four coolies ranged from Rs. 1.20 to Rs. 4.00 depending on the number of hours the rickshaw and the coolies were engaged. The rates for places outside the Municipal limits were different.

The study reported that it was possible to collect particulars of indebtedness in only a small proportion of cases but on an average 85.2 per cent rickshaw-pullers were in debt to persons in their home towns or villages. The survey pointed out the pathetic living conditions of these men and referred to the various shortcomings. Some steps were indeed taken to improve their lot but ultimately only the time came to their rescue. The decreasing number of Europeans to Simla forced them to look for alternative jobs. Now-a-days, any person riding a rickshaw is but a rare sight in Simla and the few rickshaws parked in rickshaw-sheds are gathering dust and only serve as a reminder to the Raj days. Even now no vehicle, except those of the Governor or the Chief Minister and those of fire brigade, ambulance and police are allowed on the Mall road. The traffic is restricted on almost all roads in the heart of the town. However, the residents, unlike the Europeans, prefer to walk.

The coolies and the rickshaw-pullers together constituted nearly thirty per cent of the summer population of Simla. They came mostly from Jammu and Kashmir and from the Doaba region of Punjab. They had to bear the brunt of the idiosyncrasies of the Europeans and were treated like cattle. Even the Liddells' *Simla Weekly* wrote in its issue of February 24, 1917 that the "coolie is a much abused object but he is indispensable, and though he often merits ire yet not infrequently he is treated as an animal."

The "Simla Spleen Splitting Case" attracted wide attention in 1925. A European officer is reported to have kicked a coolie in the spleen and the poor fellow had died after some days. The police initially declined to register a case but relented on pressure from the local leaders. Twenty-three coolies gave evidence in the court and the officer Mansel-Pleydell was convicted and sentenced to 18 months of rigorous imprisonment and a fine of Rs. 4,000. He committed suicide while serving his jail term.

The incident helped in organising the coolies and they formed the Balmikiyan Sweepers' Association with the backing of the Congress in 1931. Later they also waged an unsuccessful struggle to free themselves from the clutches of *choudharies*, who were given contracts to employ them and who used to charge a commission on their earnings. For a few years, the system of giving contracts to *choudharies* was abolished but they proved equally powerful and alongwith the "financiers" who were mainly traders, they forced the Municipality to re-introduce the system.

The other major class of the Indians residing in Simla during the Imperial rule was the government officials. A majority of them came with the government during the summers and went back during winters but still a considerable number were stationed at Simla permanently. They belonged to diverse regions and were put together due to compulsion of their job. Yet they tried to form groups among themselves and the British were known to encourage the tendency. It was also reflected in the number of schools and hotels that cropped up in the town mainly with a view to cater to particular groups. The very names of the schools (which were paid grants-in-aid by the local Municipal Committee) gives an idea of the presence of diverse groups. There was Sir Harcourt Butler High School, the Sanatan Dharam Sabha High School, the Islamic High School, the Madrasi Boys Primary School, the Arya Samaj Girls Middle School, the Elementary Gorkha School, the Khalsa Girls School besides the elitist Christian schools like Bishop Cotton, Auckland House, St. Edwards and Loreto Convent.

The employees, who were generally classified as 'clerks', were also paid a meagre salary. Their living conditions were bad and did not change very much during the entire Raj period. Most of them had to rent out dingy houses for exorbitant rents demanded by the landlords. They did not have roots in the town and, therefore, had little interest in its development. Thus barring some exceptions they did not settle down in Simla.

In the initial stages the 'clerks' were mainly Bengalis. Since Calcutta was the commercial and political centre where the British first arrived, the local people sought more employment with the British and had become familiar with their ways. They, however, resented the summer migration to Simla. At Calcutta these poorly paid employees had developed some other interests also and to supplement their income they had started taking tuitions or other jobs after the office hours. They were paid a meagre "Simla allowance" but were discouraged from taking their families so that the population of the town could remain in check. Most of them had to maintain two establishments and stayed in small quarters, often sharing the rooms with colleagues.

Coming from the warm climate of Calcutta they found it difficult to acclimatise in the cooler heights of Simla. *The Tribune*, in an editorial on April 30, 1883, pleaded their case and wrote that the "ill-paid and ill-fed clerks are quite unable to stand the trying cold of Simla. Surely the government ought not to inflict such hardships on them". Two of them died due to severe cold in Simla during 1884 and it led to a flurry of protest. In the subsequent years, more Punjabis and other people residing in the region were recruited as 'clerks' when the capital was shifted from Calcutta to Delhi.

They, however, did take an active interest in the exclusive socio-religious organisation which had mushroomed in the early part of this century. Thus, according to police records there were 180 government employees who were office-bearers of caste or socio-religious organisations in 1930. The organisations like the schools were mainly formed to cater to particular needs and requirements. But one trend was quite noticeable. Most of these organisations kept themselves aloof from politics, and those which began to show some interest, saw the government officials walking out of them. Partly due to the nature of their jobs and partly because they had no roots in the town, the officials avoided getting involved in politics. Though, in the meantime the number of Indian employees accompanying the government had swelled by about four times between 1921 and 1939 due to the Montague-Chelmsford reforms which led to a larger representation to Indians in government service.

The third major class, and by far the largest, was that of the shopkeepers and businessmen. Though considered the most docile class, its members began to flex their muscles first by consolidating their business in the town and later by demanding their rights which culminated in the struggle for independence. They too had come to the town to cater to the needs of the British settlers, and in the early days they used to come during the season only, but later they settled down permanently and played a major role in the development of the town.

The traders, most important among them the Sood traders who had mainly come from Kangra, were a close-knit society. In the initial stages, the two groups of Sood traders called the "newandia" and the "uchandia", who had come from the plains and the upper areas respectively; did not mix up and even intermarriage between the families belonging to the two groups was not permitted. In the course of time, however, they began mixing up and the bar on marriages was also lifted. The Sood traders held a great sway and there was a saying that the "Soods, the Sirkar and Simla" are synonymous. They also began to patronise temples and schools and one of them, Rai Sahib Nidha Mal Puran Mal became a legend in his life-time. He was a great philanthropist and helped the poor of his community with loans. He also got constructed a big *serai* for Indian travellers.

4
The Resurgence
1921–1947

The atmosphere began to grow more tense as the struggle for reform and freedom started gaining ground towards the close of the second decade and the beginning of the third decade of this century. Renewed demands were made to shift the summer capital from Simla. The town was in fact blamed by some people in England for practically everything under the sun. A letter published in *The Times* in 1917 described Simla as the town that "plunged us into the crime of the first Afghan War and into many later ill-judged and costly military enterprises, it was Simla that, only a year ago, was answerable for the Karachi troop train disaster; and it is Simla once again that is responsible for the appalling blunder and mis-management in Mesopotamia." The letter writer also quoted Sir John Kaye, who was for some time the Political Secretary to the India Office, as having described Simla as a pleasant hill sanitarium which has been the "cradle of more political insanity than any other place in the limits of Hindustan."

An editorial which appeared in *Englishman* on October 20, 1917, said: "And while the people of the plains are thus disturbed and anxious, while the atmosphere for Mr. Montague's visit grows ever more dense and electric, the governments, Imperial and provincial alike, tarry in their remote hill stations. There is one warning that recent events in India have conveyed to them in bold and unmistakable letters, but so far they have ignored it. The warning is: "Come down from your hills and govern.""

They, however, did not go down from the hills immediately. The signs, however, had begun to emerge rather clearly at the end of the second decade of the 20th century. The rise of Delhi and the shifting of the winter capital from Calcutta to Delhi partly contributed to the decline of Simla as successive Viceroys preferred to stay longer in Delhi. The growing influence of the Indians, particularly, after the decision of the Imperial Government to seek a greater association of the Indians in different branches of administration and the acceptance of a proposal to increase the representation of Indian employees in the government services leading to a consequent reduction in the number of European employees, was yet another reason why Simla fell from the favours of the British. But the single most important factor, which caused despair among the British was the growth of national awareness among the residents of Simla and the realisation that they were after all not that "docile" as they had projected themselves to be when the first Union Jack had come to the area and even during the first War of Indian Independence.

The period from the 1930s to the independence, a period of decline for the Imperial Government, saw men of great stature visit Simla. These included Mahatma Gandhi, Jawaharlal Nehru, Jinnah, Vithal Bhai Patel, Azad, Lord Mountbatten, Vallabhbhai Patel and several others. Many historians believe that the turning point for the partition of the country was reached at Simla. It was also the venue of the 1945 Simla Conference and the town where the boundaries between India and Pakistan were finally demarcated.

Mahatma Gandhi first came to Simla in May 1921. He addressed a public meeting at the Idgah which was attended by about 15,000 people. Giving his first views on Simla, he wrote, "I had heard of Simla. I had not seen the place. I often wished to see it but was always afraid to go there. I felt that I would be lost there, that I would be a barbarian among the others."

Though he liked the climate and scenic beauty of the town and said that the "Nature has withheld nothing of her riches", he was highly critical of the functioning of the government "from the 500th floor." He said that the policies framed by the Imperial Government in Simla were bad and "even the hottest parts of the country cannot give an idea of the temperature of these policies." Writing in the

Gujarati newspaper *Navajivan* on May 22, 1921, Mahatma Gandhi noted that "Simla is named after Mother Shimla as Mumbai (Bombay) is named after Mumba Devi and Calcutta after Kali. All the three Goddesses have proved faithless or, may be, the devotees have forgotten them .... After seeing Simla, my views have not changed. No end of money has been spent over the place. Even a proud man like me has had to eat humble pie. The only means of conveyance here is the horse or the rickshaw . . . the rickshaw has become quite an ordinary conveyance, as if it was the most natural thing for any of us to be yoked to a vehicle! I asked the men who pulled the rickshaw which carried me why they had taken up this work. 'Did they not have a belly to fill?' they queried in reply. I know this reply is not quite convincing; it cannot be said, though, that they take pleasure in becoming beasts of burden. On the contrary, my charge is that it is we who force men to become beasts. Why should it be surprising, then, that we have become the Empire's bullocks? . . . it is not the British alone who use the rickshaw. We use it as freely as they do. We who join them in turning people into bullocks have, therefore, become bullocks ourselves."

Mahatma Gandhi was highly critical of the functioning of the government from Simla and wrote that "so long as a distance equal to the height of 500 floors separates the Empire from us, Dyerism must need be used for maintaining the distance .... To win Swaraj means to oblige the government—whether it is British or Indian—to descend from the five hundredth floor to the ground floor and to introduce naturalness in its relations with us. The discrimination is not between white and coloured, but as between high and low."

He, however, received an unprecedented welcome by the Indian residents of Simla. He was taken in a procession with the people shouting "Betaj Badshah ki jaye" (long live the uncrowned king). He also addressed a meeting of ladies on May 14 at the Arya Samaj Hall, and according to Pamela Kanwar in her thesis, it was the first occasion that the people got the "nationalist point of view first hand."

Mahatma Gandhi again came to Simla, along with Jawaharlal Nehru, Sardar Vallabhbhai Patel, Dr. Ansari and Abdul Gaffar

Khan, in August 25, 1931 for what is called the "second settle-ment" before attending the Round Table Conference in England. An Associated Press dispatch published in the *Bombay Chronicle* dated August 27, 1931 said: "Mr. Gandhi had three hours' satis-factory talks with the Viceroy at the end of which he informed the AP that he would be sailing from Bombay for London on 29th instant. Interviewed, Mr. Gandhi declined to disclose the result of his interview (with the Viceroy) on the question of enquiry into the breaches of the pact, but said his interview was fairly satisfactory."

On his way back to 'Firgrove', Mahatma Gandhi refused to stand beyond a minute before a group of photographers at Cecil Hotel remarking: "I have no time and I cannot stand your tyranny any longer."

The nationalist spirit in Simla was catching on and the visits of the leaders further motivated and encouraged them.

The well-established traders in Simla were the people who began taking active interest in politics even as the Indian National Congress was gaining strength elsewhere in the country. Sood tra-ders and professionals, like Dr. Kedar Nath and Harish Chander, took the initiative in forming the Simla branch of the Indian National Congress in 1914, full 28 years after it was conceived by A.O. Hume in Simla town itself. The membership of the branch increased over the years but its first test came in 1919. It gave a call for a *hartal* in the town which proved to be a great success.

They then began to demand their rights and made a start with a demand for more elected members in the Simla Municipal Com-mittee. The Indian House-owners and Tax-payers' Association, which mainly constituted of the Soods who were actively involved in the Simla branch of the Indian National Congress, submitted a memorandum to seek restoration of the elective system. Since the formation of the Committee in 1852, a system was followed whereby the tax-payers had a proportionate say in the functioning of the Committee. It enabled the highest tax-payers to have the greatest influence in the working of the Committee. The House-owners in Simla, some of them owning dozens of estates, main-tained their control till 1883 when under a new policy of the government an experiment was conducted to have an elected Committee under the local self-government concept. It, however, turned into a farce when the number of members nominated by the government exceeded those of the elected and the Committee came to be virtually controlled by the nominated members.

The Indian House-owners and Tax-payers' Association also received support for its demands, for some time, by the British House-owners Association and the Punjab Traders' Association. Large public meetings and peaceful rallies were held in support of their demands and various local Congress leaders addressed the gathering. During that time several other organisations had also come into existence. Their efforts coupled with those of the local Congress leaders, yielded some results. The government agreed to review the Constitution of the Municipal Committee and it was later decided to add two elected members. This was not exactly what the Traders' Association had wished but it was a good beginning.

It was during that period that Simla witnessed another historical event. The detestable system of *begar* or forced labour had become a curse for the Indian people, particularly for the villagers and labourers. The early days of *begar* when the farmers or coolies were forced to haul up the luggage of the Europeans were over but the system was still in vogue for arduous jobs or where voluntary labour was not available. Worse still, was the practice of picking up villagers for *begar* to help the *sahib bahadurs* in *shikar*. The European settlers in Simla often invited friends and other influential people for hunting and picnics and asked their menials to arrange for free service of the natives who were compelled to serve as labourers and porters.

The Europeans had taken the *begar* system for granted. While on official tours, the Europeans were entitled to depend entirely on *begar* for transport and supply of necessary articles of food. The *lumberdar* had to perform the functions of a tour superintendent if any British official visited his village. He had to look after the supply of food stuff and also arrange transportation from his own village to the next camp. They had no choice in the matter. *The Tribune*, in an editorial published on February 10, 1921 pointed out that "one of the fruitful causes of discontent

among some of the most backward communities of upper India
and the Punjab is the inequitous system of *begar* or forced labour
which not only prevails in the hilly districts of Simla and Kumaon
but even in rural areas in the plains . . . it is neither in the interest of government nor of the people that there should be more
discontent than can possibly be helped. The *begar* system is cruel
and mischievous and, therefore, a dangerous anachronism which
should be abolished root and branch without delay."

The struggle against *begar* in Simla was spearheaded by
Samuel Evans Stokes, who had migrated from America and was
later responsible for introducing apple in the region. He had
remained aloof from politics and had remained a supporter of the
Imperial Government. However, during World War I, he offered
his services to the government and acted as recruiting agent for
the army at Kotgarh. This brought him into close contact with
the villagers and the system of *begar* struck him as most repre-
hensible. He wrote several letters and sent numerous representa-
tions to the authorities to put a ban on the system but to no effect.
He wrote that "we have to find a way in which foreign officials
live, as inaccessible as Mahadeva on Mount Kailash, each surrounded by his vortex of parasites who fatten upon the miseries
of a poor and inarticulate peasantry."

He mobilised the villagers who had been suffering from this
system since several decades. He held several meetings with the
local authorities and the Simla branch of Indian National Congress
backed the demand for the abolition of the system of *begar*. Ultimately, after a series of meetings and discussions, the government
agreed to abolish the system in Simla Hills in September 1921.
It was another landmark in the movement to demand due rights
for the Indians.

A little after the system was abolished, Stokes withdrew himself from active politics and devoted himself to the development
of apple cultivation in the area. The Congress also went through
a period of hibernation till it was revived in 1929. In between,
Simla attracted several leaders and it was during this period that
the Legislative Assembly building or the Council Chamber was
constructed in 1925—the last important building to be built during the Raj days.

The Council Chamber, which was opened by Lord Reading on August 21, 1925, has remained witness to history taking shape in Simla since then. The building constructed at a cost of Rs. 8.5 lakhs, has seen the era of Vithal Bhai Patel whose conduct of the proceedings is still remembered with reverence. The chair occupied by him is now occupied by the Speaker of the Himachal Pradesh Vidhan Sabha. It was this Council Chamber which heard the "thunder of Satyamurti and Bhula Bhai Desai and witnessed the debating talent of Moti Lal Nehru and Mohammad Ali Jinnah." The *Chronicle* had written an interesting piece about the historical Council Chamber. It reported that before the government decided to build the Chamber, Sir Claudehill, who was then the Public Works Member, took special pains to ascertain the views of the then Legislature. He appointed a Committee of 15 representatives from all parts of the country and discussed the question in great details. Only one member opposed the idea of the building in Simla, and when Sir George Lounders asked him why he preferred sessions in Delhi in hot weather, he replied that he would not be present at them as he had no intention of joining the new Assembly.

After the partition the East Punjab Government shifted to Simla and its assembly held sessions in the Council Chamber. This was continued till 1953 when the assembly was shifted to Chandigarh in its newly constructed premises. After the shifting of the Punjab Assembly, the Assembly of the part 'C' State of Himachal Pradesh, which till then used to hold its meetings in the Viceregal Lodge (re-named Rashtrapati Niwas), was given the hall for its meetings.

But the building was to see varied periods. In 1955 the lower portion of the building was allotted to the All India Radio for setting up a 2.5 KV shortwave station. The Council Chamber fell on evil days when Himachal Assembly was dissolved on October 31, 1956 after the report of the State Re-organisation Commission and the Himachal Pradesh became a Union Territory under an administrator who was designated as Lieutenant Governor. On May 5, 1957, the building (former 'Foreign Office Building') in which the Himachal Administrative Secretariat was located, was destroyed in a big fire. As a temporary measure the offices of the government had to be shifted to the Council Chamber. Thus the building saw the re-construction of the partly burnt records of Himachal Pradesh and the Chief Secretary occupied the room which is now the office of the Speaker of the Legislative Assembly.

Life was brought back to the Council Chamber hall with the restoration of the legislature to Himachal Pradesh on July 1, 1963. It was only later in 1966 that Himachal Pradesh was granted full statehood and Simla regained the status of capital of a State.

The visits of the stalwarts of the various leaders to Simla to attend the Assembly meeting provided an impetus to the political activity in the town. The membership of the party rose sharply partly due to the efforts of the local Congress leaders who wanted to get representation to the Provincial Congress Committee. The membership of Congress in Simla, according to the police records of that period rose from just 67 in 1929 to 411 in 1925. Simultaneously a large number of organisations of labourers and workers came into existence which had large memberships. These organisations included the Rickshaw Coolies' Association and the Balmikiyan Sweepers' Association. A Kashmiri Muslim Labour Board also came into existence and the secretary of the Simla branch of the Congress, Omar Nomani was elected as its general secretary.

April 26, 1930 was a momentous day in Simla. Vithal Bhai Patel, who was the president of the Legislative Assembly resigned from his post at Simla. This sparked off civil disobedience in the town. He was taken in a procession around the town and through the Mall road by a 2,000 strong crowd. The processionists raised slogans in favour of the Congress and against the government. This was the biggest demonstration staged in Simla during that period and the Imperial lords were left in little doubt about the coming of age of Congress in Simla. Perhaps the most disturbing aspect of the procession for them was the participation of a large number of Indian employees who had, hitherto, remained aloof from active politics. As part of the civil disobedience and transgression of rules, 53 Congress workers were arrested during May, June and July in 1930.

Besides the movement at the national level, Simla was also rife with the activities of the members of Praja Mandals. The organisations were, in a way, the outcome of the revival of the Simla branch of the Indian National Congress. The All India State's People's Conference at Ludhiana provided an impetus to activate the Praja Mandals. A large number of Congress leaders were in the forefront of the movement. Unlike the struggle for the abolition of *begar*, which started from the areas away from Simla and which later moved to the town, the Praja Mandals owe their existence to Simla and subsequently the movement spread to the adjoining areas. Simla was made the base for launching and coordinating the struggle. In May 1939, the Himalayan State's People's Conference held a function and the decision of using Simla as a focal point to coordinate the struggle was taken. As a sequel, the Himalaya Riasti Praja Mandal was launched at Simla with Pandit Padam Dev as the president on June 1, 1939. The organisation tasted its first success when the Rana of Kunihar accepted its demand on July 9, 1939.

The ruler of Dhami, a small state about 15 kilometres from Simla, however, declined to accept the demand. Certain old residents of the area still remember the days when the Viceroy and his entourage used to visit the area for *shikar*. An area of 2,355 acres was reserved for the annual hunting expedition by the Viceroy in Dhami State. Bhagmal Sauhta, one of the leading members of the Praja Mandal movement, formed the Shri Dhami Prem Pracharni Sabha on June 1, 1939. A general meeting of Dhami residents was held on July 13 and it was decided to stage a demonstration on July 16. A day prior to the scheduled date, the Dhami Durbar issued an order under Section 144 of the State Criminal Procedure Code prohibiting Bhagmal from entering the State. On July 16 he was stopped by the Dhami State Police at Ghanahatti and taken into custody when he insisted on visiting Halog, the capital of the State. The policemen took him to Halog for detention. A huge crowd gathered and formed a procession to Halog. The sight of the Rana of Dhami and the rumour that he would order firing caused a melee. The agitation took a violent turn and the armed guard with the Rana resorted to firing.

Later during the course of an inquiry, the government found that a large number of persons who had taken part in the agitation were low-paid government employees. This revelation came as a rude shock to the government which had considered them to be non-political. The employees had generally refrained from taking part in such activity and were considered docile. The only known incident involving government employees in Simla prior to the Dhami incident, was the spontaneous participation of some employees in a procession soon after Vithal Bhai Patel had resigned from the Legislative Assembly. That incident was, however, considered a fluke and a result of emotional outburst.

Subsequently, the Praja Mandal Movement spread to certain other areas also, notably in Suket and Paghasta where Vaid Surat Singh led the agitation.

The increase in political activities led the Imperial Government to tighten the security arrangements around Simla. A thorough checking and verification of antecedents of persons coming to Simla was carried out in the garb of medical checkup. Three plague check points were established at Tara Devi, the railway station and the motor stand. Dr. B.R. Nanda recalls that he had himself undergone the experience several times. All Indians were asked their name, father's name, the place from where they were coming, the place they wished to go and the reasons for the journey. He says that the checking was carried out on the excuse that persons with contagious diseases should not enter Simla. However, he says, the police at Simla were tipped about "suspects" and those found to have links with political or militant organisations were summarily asked to go back. At one occasion the then general secretary of the Simla unit of the Congress, Nand Lal Verma refused to give his particulars at the Tara Devi checkpost and was taken into custody.

Dr. Nanda, whose clinic in the Lower Bazar was at one time also the official clinic for Burmese railways, recalls that Simla was the headquarters of the exiled Burma Government from July 1942 to 1945. He says that the Burmese were particularly nice with the Indians in contrast to the condescending attitude of the British. He recalls that the various offices of the exiled government were scattered in different buildings in Simla. The Army Headquarters building, which had been vacated after the Imperial Army Headquarter was shifted to Delhi in 1941, was almost entirely placed at the disposal of the exiled Burmese Government. Other offices were located in buildings like the Royal Hotel, the Willows Bank and the Longwood where they were engaged "in the reconstruction of post-war Burma."

Coming back to the security aspect. While a close look was maintained at people coming to Simla, the Imperial Government also imposed restrictions on the khadi-clad Congress workers and "other ill-dressed" Indians moving on the Mall. The Municipality had earlier restricted the entry of porters to the Mall road during day time. Ironically, this still applies on the Mall road and the porters still have to take a long circuit if they are engaged during the restricted hours. However, the restriction on people wearing khadi led to wide resentment and in 1930 several Congress workers courted arrest for defying the orders when they picketed shops on the Mall under Gandhiji's anti-liquor movement. The police sent 126 workers for trial and 100 of them were convicted.

A militant organisation, called the Bal Bharat Sabha, was established by a Sood trader named Dina Nath "Andhi". He courted arrest several times and was among the demonstrators who were dispersed with the help of the fire brigade which was ordered to turn the water hose on them in August 1930. During his interrogation by the police he gave his name as "Andhi, son of Gandhi". He later joined the Congress Socialist Party. The British rulers, faced with increasing protests, further strengthened their police and intelligence wing.

The same attitude of the British rulers was reflected in the functioning of the Municipality. The annual report of the Simla Municipal Committee contained a new column from 1938. It was meant for the Deputy Commissioner, who was the ex-officio president of the Municipal Committee, to report on the "general attitude of members towards their responsibilities, how far they were actuated by personal or party motives and how far they are dependent on official initiative." Such actions also led to the decreasing number of "moderates" in the town.

The landlords and traders in Simla received a jolt when it was decided to reduce the strength of government employees coming to Simla during the summer. The funds sanctioned for the development of Simla were also withdrawn that year. In 1925, the government permitted the British officers to spend their holidays in England. All this led to a crash in the rents and a slump in business at Simla.

The report on the administration of the Simla Municipality for the year 1940-41 pointed out that "the curtailment of exodus of the Government of India (has) affected a large number of houses in the bazar area which remained vacant and the Committee had to grant remission of taxes on 548 houses in the first moiety and on 302 houses for the second moiety which resulted in the reduction of income under house and water taxes amounting to about Rs. 17,000."

The decision to drastically reduce the number of officials accompanying the government and the curtailment of duration of stay of the government came in for severe criticism from the House-owners and Merchants' Association of Simla. Its president, Sir Jai Lal did not mince words when, in his speech delivered to the members of the Association, he said that the decisions of the government are "unsound and uneconomical to the government itself" and pointed out that the decisions were made on the "professed ground that only as many officials will move up to Simla as can find accommodation here. It is well known that, in spite of the fact that the number of officials has been much increased owing to the war and comparatively a large number of European visitors have come to Simla, many houses are still vacant."

He said that while the decision had seriously affected the house-owners and merchants of Simla, it has also led to a reduction in the income of the Municipal Committee. He stressed that "there seems to be an impression abroad that there is still the same difficulty in securing good accommodation in Simla as used to be experienced in the previous years. This is wrong." He also advised the house-owners to improve the condition of their houses on modern lines. He, however, struck an optimistic note by saying that he believed that "in spite of the present depressing circumstances there is a great future for Simla. No other hill station in India can provide the same facilities for travel comfort and health as Simla can, but a little enterprise is needed on the part of the Municipal Committee and, of course, of the house-owners, to attract a large number of visitors and to provide a variety of conveniences and amusements to them." Thus the house-owners and traders seemed to have virtually given up hope for the government to move to the hills in full strength again.

The decline in the importance of Simla also cast its reflection in the working of the Municipality. Several schemes were simply dragged on unlike the quick implementation as in the past. The funds at its disposal were not properly and fully utilised and in one year alone it had returned Rs. five lakhs unspent to the government. The Municipality, in its report in 1940-41, admitted that the improvement schemes have not made any "appreciable progress" and also that "the Municipality was not inspected by the Commissioner or any other government officer during the year."

Vere Birdwood has mentioned in her book an instance of the attitude of escapism and indifference growing among the British officers. Quoting from a series of minutes she saw in 1941, which were added to a file, she wrote that "the most junior officer had written. 'I don't think we'd better start this project, there may not be time to finish it.' His senior officer had noted, 'what nonsense. I was told this in 1919.' And the Governor had noted on the same file, 'absolute nonsense, I was told this in 1909'."

Renewed demands were made to convert the Municipality into a wholly elective body with a nominated president following the unsatisfactory decision to increase the number of elected members from three to five. Sir Jai Lal said that "the only ground advanced by the government for retaining this archaic constitution is that it owns much property in Simla" and added that "actually the government pays only 33 per cent of the taxes. He said that with the limited number of elected members the Muslims and the Sikhs do not get proper representation. He said that the Muslims were keen to have a separate electorate system for which "we would not object though we consider the system obnoxious to good government."

He asserted that the house-owners and the traders had a "vital stake" in the property and business in the town because they are the permanent residents of the town and that they should be given an "effective voice". He pleaded that "if they cannot give us a more popular constitution" it would be in the interest of Simla that the government should directly assume responsibility for the administration of the town.

Little did he know that the Municipal Committee, which was later converted into a Municipal Corporation, shall have to wait for no less than twenty-five years in independent India to have an effective and fully elected body. This too was done on the intervention of courts after some public spirited persons had filed a writ petition. The elections to the Corporation were held in 1986 after successive governments avoided to get themselves involved in the institution of local self-government.

Simla was the venue of some of the most important events in the years immediately preceding 1947, which moulded the history of the sub-continent. The chain of events started in 1945 when the town was the venue for the well-known Simla conference. The then Viceroy, Lord Wavell announced that it was his intention to hold a political conference in Simla "to ease the present political situation and to advance India towards her goal of full self-government." The purpose of the conference was the formation of a new Executive Council, which had been debated rather hotly for the last several years, and which would be "more representative of organised political opinion." It was hoped that the new Council would give due representation to Hindus and Muslims. It was proposed that it would be entirely an Indian Council except for the Viceroy and the Commander-in-Chief who would hold charge of the defence portfolio.

Lord Wavell made his proposals known on June 14, 1945 and a round of hectic political activity started. The leaders of Hindus and Muslims met several times to reach a consensus. Even Mahatma Gandhi and Jinnah met to discuss the issue. Some difference of opinion had cropped up even when the proposals were made. *The Tribune*, in an editorial on June 16, 1945 sounded sceptic of the Wavell Plan and said that "it will be deceiving oneself to imagine that the Wavell Plan will either appease the hunger of the people of India for freedom or it will bring India much nearer the realisation of her objective for which lakhs of her sons have undergone great sufferings and made untold sacrifices. . . not only is the scheme disappointing, but it may even prove dangerous to the growth of both a healthy, democratic state in India and a united Indian nation. The danger lies in the introduction of communal representation in the Executive Council on the basis of equal representation of Hindus, who constitute more than 50 per cent of the population, and the Muslims who constitute less than 25 per cent of the population . . . ".

Twenty-one invitees assembled in the Viceregal Lodge at Simla on June 25, 1945 at 11 A.M. It was perhaps one of the most crucial meetings before independence and the attention of the entire country, and even of the world, was focused on the Viceregal Lodge from where an important step toward the sub-continent's future was to be taken. The members of the conference were Abul Kalam Azad, president of the Congress, P.N. Banerjee, leader of the Nationalist Party in the Legislative Assembly, Bhula Bhai Desai, leader of the Congress Party in the Legislative Assembly, Sir Ghulam Hussain Hidayatullah, premier of Sind, Hossain Imam, leader of the Muslim League party in the Council of States, Mohammed Ali Jinnah, president of the Muslim League, Liaqat Ali Khan, deputy leader of the Muslim League in the Indian Legislative Assembly, Khizr Hyat Khan, premier of the Punjab, B.G. Kher, former premier of Bombay, G.S. Motilal, leader of the Congress Party in the Council of States, Khawaja Sir Nazimuddin, former premier of Bengal, Pandit Govind Ballabh Pant, former premier of the United Provinces, the Maharaja of Barla Kimadi, former premier of Orissa, C. Rajagopalachari, former premier of Madras, Sir Henry Richardson, leader of the European group in the Legislative Assembly, Sir Mahomed Saidullah, premier of Assam, Dr. Khan Sahib, premier of the Northwest frontier province, Ravi Shankar Shukla, former premier of the Central Province, Master Tara Singh, Sri Krishna Sinha, former premier of Bihar, and N. Sivaraj.

Mahatma Gandhi, whom the Viceroy had invited to the conference, had declined to paticipate in it but had promised to be in Simla during the course of the conference. Accordingly he stayed in Simla and remained in close touch with the participating Congress Party members.

The Viceroy in his opening address underlined the importance of the conference and said that, "the statesmanship, wisdom and goodwill of all of us is here on trial, not merely in the eyes of Indians but before the whole world." The Viceroy also asked the members to keep the proceedings confidential. The sittings of the conference were not open to the press but at the end of each day a press statement was issued with the approval of the members. Sir Even Jenkins and V.P. Menon were appointed as secretaries to the conference.

The conference, however, reached a deadlock over the composition of the Executive Council. There was a stalemate when Jinnah insisted that only the members of the Muslim League should be considered against the reservation for Muslims in the Council. This implied that even Maulana Abul Kalam Azad, the president of the Congress could not be a member of the Executive Council. The Congress wanted a right to include in its quota, members from all communities including the Muslims, Christians and the Scheduled Castes. On June 27 it was agreed that the meeting should be adjourned so that Jinnah and Pant could continue informal talks to arrive at a solution. The meeting was adjourned till June 29. But when the conference met that day, it was evident that the Congress and the Muslim League had failed in reaching any agreement. Jinnah also met the Viceroy separately to explain to him that he cannot agree to the appointment of Muslims who were not members of Muslim League to the Executive Council but said that he would be prepared to consider any new formula proposed by the Viceroy.

The Viceroy then decided to intervene directly and began preparing a list of representatives of different communities who could be inducted to the Executive Council. The conference was adjourned till July 14. The intervening period also saw hectic political activity in Simla and the Indian leadership ventured to strike out a compromise formula to avoid the hovering clouds of the partition of the country. Jawaharlal Nehru was also called to Simla for consultations and "Simla was almost mad with enthusiasm" on his arrival, as Jagat S. Bright put it in his *Life of Jawaharlal Nehru*.

Both the Congress and the Muslim League convened meetings of their respective working committees to consider a fresh proposal of the Viceroy about the submission of lists. The Muslim League adopted a tough strategy and decided not to submit any list. V.P. Menon, one of the secretaries to the conference who later rose to the position of constitutional Adviser to the Governor-General and several other important posts writes in his *The Trans-*

fer of Power in India that the Viceroy and Gandhiji met on July 11 and the Viceroy informed him that "in view of the unwillingness of the Muslim League to cooperate, except on its own terms, the conference had failed."

Efforts were made to save the conference from failure even at the eleventh hour. Menon giving an eye-witness account in his book writes that, "even after it was known that Jinnah had refused to submit his list, hope persisted that the Viceroy would find a way out. This sentiment was not confined to any particular school of thought or opinion. For instance, just before the Viceroy communicated his final decision to the members, Hossain Imam, who attended the conference in his capacity as a leader of the Muslim League party in the Council of States, stopped me on my way to the Cecil Hotel and confided to me his feeling of distress over the imminent breakdown. He urged me even at that late hour to see Liaqat Ali Khan in order to find a way out of the impasse. He gave me the impression that the members of the working committee of the Muslim League were far from unanimous in rejecting the Viceroy's offer. Hossain Imam suggested that the Viceroy was not aware that a member of his own Executive Council was advising Jinnah to stand firm. On arrival at the Cecil Hotel, I telephoned to Liaqat Ali Khan, who readily agreed to meet me. I discussed the general situation with him that evening, stressing some of the dangers that would overtake the country if any agreement was not reached. He gave me the impression that the crucial issue with the League was the insufficiency of the Viceroy's vote to protect Muslim interests."

"Liaqat Ali told me that he would consult Jinnah and let me know his reaction the next day. I never heard from him . . . the conference at Simla had been conceived as a gathering of politically eminent persons who would sit together and collectively advise the Viceroy about the formation of a new Central Government. Very soon, however, it became transformed into the familiar pattern of futile discussions between the Congress and the Muslim League and between big party leaders and the Viceroy. The formal sessions of the conference served as the forum for party leaders to set out their points of view whilst members functioned as the audience or chorus. Rajagopalachari made pointed reference to this in a statement soon after the conference ended".

On July 14 at the fifth and the last session of the conference, the Viceroy accepted his full responsibility for the failure of the conference. In his speech, the Viceroy said that in view of the stand taken by the Muslim League, the conference has failed. "Nobody can regret this more than I do myself. I wish to make it clear that the responsibility for the failure is mine. The main idea underlying the conference was mine. If it had succeeded, its success would have been attributed to me and I cannot place the blame for its failure upon any of the parties."

He appealed to the party leaders to "accept this view, and to do all they can to ensure that there are no recriminations. It is of the utmost importance that this effort to secure agreement between the parties and communities should not result in a worsening of communal feelings. I ask you all to exercise the greatest possible restraint." He ended his speech by saying that "do not any of you be discouraged by this setback. We shall overcome our difficulties in the end. The future greatness of India is not in doubt."

Writes Menon, "the Simla conference afforded a last opportunity to the forces of nationalism to fight a rear-guard action to preserve the integrity of the country, and when the battle was lost the waves of communalism quickly engulfed it. Only the Hobson's choice of partition was left."

The Simla conference marked an important watershed in the history of the country and it had a deep impact on events leading to the partition. It was at this conference, some historians assert, that Lord Wavell formally gave the veto power to Jinnah. The deadlock provided strength to the Muslim League and weakened those Muslims who were not members of the League. The historians are divided, as on several other things, about who was at fault. While most Hindus and Congress believed that the League had adopted a rigid attitude and was at fault, others blamed the Congress. Some observers allege that a statement made by Jawaharlal Nehru to the press that in case of any difference of opinion in the Council, the majority verdict would be binding, further hardened the attitude of the Muslim League and led to the failure of the conference.

In their book *The Partition of India*, C.H. Philips and M.D. Wainwright observe that "the Congress, instead of reaching an understanding with the Muslims on the basis of parity, denied the latter's right to represent the Muslims and insisted on claiming seats out of the Muslim quota. Thus another opportunity for a smooth transfer of power by mutual consent was lost due to Congress's incorrigible tendency to grab power to the detriment of other elements."

The following year, from May 5 to 12, 1946, another historical meeting took place between the Cabinet Mission and the representatives of the Congress and the Muslim League. The Congress was represented by Jawaharlal Nehru, Azad, Vallabhbhai Patel and Abdul Gaffar Khan. The Muslim League was represented by Jinnah, Mahommed Ismail Khan, Liaqat Ali Khan, and Abdur Rab Nishtar. But it was again headed for a failure. The disagreement between the two parties proved too wide to be reconciled The conference met finally on May 12 for a short session and it was agreed that no useful purpose would be served by its continuation.

Before the eventual partition and independence of the country, Simla was again the venue of some important events. The first one was in May 1947 when the then Viceroy Lord Louis Mountbatten arrived to decide about the future of the country. He was also waiting for the approval of a plan he had submitted to the British Government for an honourable exit of Britishers from India. Larry Collins and Dominique Lapierre in their well-known *Freedom at Midnight* have given a graphic description of the event at Simla and the reaction of Jawaharlal to the proposal of Lord Mountbatten. They wrote that the Viceroy was quite confident of the eventual acceptance of a plan prepared by him which had been modified by the British Government in England. They wrote that "Mountbatten had inserted in the plan a clause which would allow an Indian province to become independent if a majority of both its communities wished it. That clause was intended to provide that the 65 million Hindus and Muslims of Bengal could unite into one viable country with the great sea-port of Calcutta as a capital."

While waiting for the final approval of the plan, Lord Mountbatten also sent his senior officer, V.P. Menon to discuss the issue with Nehru who was in Simla but forbid him from disclosing the plan sent by him to the British Government. Menon did not mention anything about the proposals to Nehru but reported back to Mountbatten that his proposals were not likely to be accepted by the Congress. Lord Mountbatten did not take his suggestion seriously but later he had a "hunch" and he decided to sound Nehru on the proposals. Accordingly he sent for Nehru and asked him to take a copy of the proposals and to study them over-night.

Nehru returned to his suite, which was located in the Vice-regal Lodge itself and, as Collins and Lapierre write, "a few hours later, while Mountbatten devoted himself to his regular evening relaxation, constructing his family's geneaological table, Jawaharlal Nehru began to scrutinize the text designed to chart his country's future. He was horrified by what he read. The vision of India that emerged from the plan's pages was a nightmare, an India divided, not into two parts, but fragmented into a dozen pieces. The door Mountbatten had left open for Bengal would become, Nehru foresaw, a world through which the best blood of India would pour. He saw India deprived of its lungs, the port of Calcutta alongwith its mills, factories, steelworks; Kashmir, his beloved Kashmir, an independent State ruled by a despot he despised; Hyderabed become an enormous, indigestible Moslim body planted in the belly of India; half a dozen other princely States clamouring to go off on their own. The plan, he believed, would exacerbate all India's fissiperous tendencies—dialect, culture, race—to the point at which the sub-continent would risk exploding into a mosaic of weak, hostile states."

Nehru's reaction after reading the proposals was, obviously, furious. He discussed the proposals with Krishna Menon and drafted an angry letter which was delivered to Viceroy the next morning. Collins and Lapierre, who claim to have gathered the account first hand from Mountbatten, Krishna Menon and through the daughter of V.P. Menon, write in their inimitable style, "reading Nehru's words, the poised, self-assured Viceroy who'd proudly announce to the world that he was going to present a solution to India's dilemma in ten days' time, suddenly realised he had no solution at all. The plan he'd assured Attlee would win Indian acceptance, would never get passed by the one element in India that had to accept it, the Congress Party."

The Viceroy was at a crucial stage of his life and had to find a way out. He summoned V.P. Menon and told him that "by that evening, he would have to re-draft the Charter that would give India her independence. Its essential option, partition, had to remain and it must above all continue to place the responsibility for making a choice upon the Indians themselves through the vote of their provincial assemblies. Menon finished his task in accordance with Mountbatten's instructions. The man who had begun his career as a two-finger typist culminated it by re-drafting, in barely six hours in an office porch looking out on the Himalayas a plan which was going to re-order the sub-continent and alter the map of the world."

In Menon's own words Lord Mountbatten "told me that he had shown the draft plan to Nehru and he was not sorry that he had done so." He reminiscenses that he returned to his hotel and "I had only two or three hours in which to prepare an alternative draft plan and I sat to work on it at once." The Viceroy was anxious to show the draft to Nehru and to ascertain his reactions before he left Simla that evening, and I had barely got the draft into shape when Sir Eric Mieville came and took it away to the Viceroy. "That night I dined at the Viceregal Lodge. I found that Lord Mountbatten had completely regained his buoyant spirits and good cheer. He told me that he had shown the draft to Nehru, who had said that the approach contained in it was on proper lines and it would not be unacceptable to the Congress."

And finally when it was decided that the country would be partitioned, a Boundary Commission was appointed with Sir Cyril Radcliffe as Chairman of the two Commissions for Bengal and Punjab. Each Commission constituted of the Chairman and two members from each community. The members for the Punjab Commission were Mr. Justice Mehr Chand Mahajan, Teja Singh, Din Mahomed and Muhammad Munir. The Commission held meetings in a room in the Lahore High Court and continued sittings till the end of July.

Mr. Justice Mahajan, in his book *Looking Back*, writes that "after our sittings in Lahore were over, we were taken to Simla under police escort and lodged in the Cecil Hotel for the writing of our report." The last meeting of the Boundary Commission, according to Mr. Justice Mahajan, was again held in the United Services Club, which coincidently, was also the place where the Macmohan Line was drawn several decades ago. He further writes that Sir Radcliffe presided over the last meeting of the Commission and said: "Gentlemen, you have disagreed and therefore the duty falls on me to give the award which I will do later on".

Neither Lord Mountbatten nor the members of the Commission were aware of the final award till it was announed on August 17. Sir Radcliffe was ready with his award only on August 13 and Lord Mountbatten had planned to handover the copies of the award to the Congress and the Muslim League immediately after he had received it. But since he was going to Karachi on August 13 he could not possibly summon the party leaders on that date. The earliest he could meet them was on his return on August 16 and copies were handed over to the two parties on that day at Delhi. As was feared, the Radcliffe award satisfied none of the parties but both sides agreed that the award may be accepted for the time being and amendments may be made later through negotiations.

The relations between the two major communities in Simla, the Hindus and the Muslims, had began to turn sour as a direct result of the animosity between the Congress and the Muslim League at the national level. Since the very inception of the town the two communities had together helped its growth and had developed close family ties. In fact, the caste Hindus preferred to exchange things and purchase articles from the Muslims rather than from the "low-caste" Hindus. The relations of *Dharam bhai* and *Dharam behan* were quite common. They had been together through all the difficulties, humiliations at the hands of the British rulers and the sorrows and joys. None of them, as indeed no one, actually belonged to the area. They had all come in view of the growing importance of the town and to cater to the needs of the population. A substantial number of Muslims, like Hindus, were traders, artisans and porters. People belonging to both the communities were in the employment of the Imperial Government and no old records had mentioned any dispute or clash on communal lines in Simla.

The postures of the Congress and the Muslim League, which suited the rulers for their "divide and rule policy" created suspicion among the communities in Simla as at other places. The Muslims in Simla also began to demand more representation in the Municipality which was opposed by the Hindus. The much publicised, Ram Devi Abduction Case in 1934, widened the gulf which could not be bridged again till the partition. A Hindu woman was reportedly abducted by two Kashmiri Muslim men. She was later recovered but the episode was given a communal colour.

By the time it became known that the country is being partitioned, the situation had worsened in Simla. Tension was apparent in the town and the people belonging to the two communities preferred to move in groups. The reports, more importantly the rumours, added to the tension. Muslims began to muster strength and the rumours were rife that they were planning an attack. The Rashtriya Swayam Sewak Sangh (R.S.S.), which had been established in Simla in the early forties, also got activated. A massive gathering was organised by the R.S.S. at the Annandale ground and, according to eye-witnesses, about 4,000 Hindus participated in camp.

R.K. Kaushal, who is one of the eye-witnesses to those days, says that the show of strength by the R.S.S. helped substantially in the days to come. Though it was considered a non-political organisation, the Simla branch of the R.S.S. "helped to balance the influence of the Muslims" which resulted in avoiding any major conflagration. The Muslims began to fortify themselves in the Elysium Hotel (now Government Girls College), the Metropole and the Masjid in the Lower Bazar. They were given full protection by the administration. Deputy Commissioner Mr. Kewal Singh as well as the majority of the Municipal Committee members, who were Muslims helped to control the situation. In fact the Muslims as well as the Hindus had began shifting their families to safer places soon after it was known that the partition was imminent.

Mangat Dhani, who was the leader of the 18 evening branches or *Shakhas* of the R.S.S. in Simla, however, says that the massive gathering at Annandale had nothing to do with any planning to attack the Muslims. He says that at no meeting anyone thought of organising riots or attacking the Muslims and adds that the morale of the Hindus was quite low at that time in Simla and the meeting was organised to "boost the sagging morale of the Hindus." He recolleçts that "there were fanatics on both sides" and some extremist elements among Muslims, who were mainly employees with little contact with the local population, used to move in hordes creating panic among the Hindu shopkeepers. The R.S.S. organised route-marches "but did not at any time think of organising the raid", he asserts. He admits that certain Hindus and Sikh fanatics looted and burnt some shops but the victims, he says, were only those "who preached fanaticism." About half a dozen lives were lost despite tight security arrangements.

In the *Plain Tales from the Raj*, one Sylvia Corfield has been quoted as a witness to those days in Simla. She recalls the day as she waited in Simla for a military convoy to take her to safety and watched "all the shops being looted. I remember standing in the verandah of the United Services Club which had opened its doors to women, standing there with the Bishop of Lahore and hearing the rickshaw coolies' quarters in the Lower Bazar being bombed. We felt quite helpless listening to their cries and the dull thud of the explosions. We could'nt do anything. . . ."

The same book gives an account by Fay Campbell-Johnson, wife of Mountbatten's press attache, who "gaped in horror at the spectacle she beheld from the verandah of Cecil Hotel where the Raj's summering rulers had sipped their tea. Sikhs on bicycles, waving their kirpans, were swooping down the Mall chasing fleeing Muslims like hunters a fox. They would ride up behind a gasping victim and behead him with one terrible swish of their swords."

Many eye-witnesses to those days, some of whom are still in government service at Simla, believe that these accounts were highly exaggerated. They say that only sporadic incidents did take place "between the fanatics" on both sides but the situation did not worsen and there was no organised attack. Even the official reports do not mention any such attack. In one incident, recalls an eye-witness, the hand of a Himachali youth was chopped off by some persons in the belief that he was a Muslim.

But while some unfortunate incidents took place, a large number of acts and gestures of goodwill have not been recorded. Mian Goverdhan Singh, who was an eye-witness to one such incident, recalls that his father Mian Joban Das, a *vakil* to the erstwhile Raja of Jubbal, had a close friend in Mehad Ali Shah who was at that time a vice-president of the Simla Municipality. Mehad Ali Shah, like other Muslims, was forced to seek shelter in a camp at Kalka and he left some of his articles with Mian Joban Das's family while he himself was away. On his return, Mian Joban Das was informed about his friend. He realised that his friend must be in great difficulty and might not have been able to take cash and jewellery with him.

He at once decided to leave for Kalka to meet his friend and to provide him the necessary help. His family members dissuaded him and pointed out the danger inherent in a journey to Kalka during those troubled times. However, he had decided to go. He disguised himself, borrowed some money from the then Raja of Jubbal, and set out in a motor for Kalka. With great difficulty he was able to locate his friend and handed over to him cash and jewellery. Several years later, when Mian Joban Das died in an accident, Mehad Ali Shah wrote feelingly about their friendship and gratefully remembered his gesture in those difficult times.

Mian Goverdhan Singh also recounts an incident in Kumbra village in Jubbal which had a large concentration of Muslims. The village was surrounded by Hindu-dominated villages. His uncle, sensing danger, provided shelter to all Muslims in his house and arranged for their safe transportation to the camps. Several of them returned to the village after the return of normalcy and hold his uncle in high esteem. There were many number of incidents where Hindus, who had developed strong bonds with their Muslim brethren over the decades, faced danger but came to their rescue. Though sporadic incidents could not be stopped, the town was spared the agony of organised violence.

The single-most important factor which saved Simla from being the scene of bloodbath was the fact that unlike in the plains, where villagers came to the towns and engaged in massacre and rioting, or the people of one *muhalla* acted similarly against the residents of another *muhalla*, Simla had no large settlements in the villages around it. The town also did not have any *mohalla* and the population, which is more prone to get involved during such times, was concentrated in the Lower Bazar areas. The old ties built over the generations prevented any major clash among the residents of the area and no outsider could infiltrate to disrupt the situation. At the height of the emotion-charged days, however, almost all Muslims were shifted to camps. Only a handful came back when the things had cooled down and they were treated as fellow citizens.

Another factor, which saved the residents of Simla from any gruesome tragedy, was the fact that it was isolated from the sensitive areas and any group planning to launch an offensive on the town had to travel over hundred kilometres. Firstly, no one could have thus dared to travel such a distance during those days and, secondly, any such group could have been easily spotted on way from Kalka. The initial British strategy to choose the area from the point of view of security, ultimately helped in saving the town from a ghastly scene during the dreadful days of the partition.

5
A New Era
1947–1987

The dawn of Indian independence saw Simla as the capital of what was then called East Punjab. The Indian tricolour was unfurled outside 'Ellerslie', the Secretariat of the Punjab Government which is now the Himachal Pradesh Government Secretariat. Thousands of people, including those from the neighbouring villages, converged on the main road outside the 'Ellerslie' to participate in the historic function. There are still many people in the town who remember the event vividly. The function continued for several hours as people sang and danced to welcome Independence. A procession was also taken out through the town and there were many who felt sad at the absence of Muslims and at their vacant houses. Very few Europeans were left in the town and they too were preparing to leave. No one cared to remember the Viceregal Lodge over which the Union Jack had flown for nearly sixty years as a symbol of British rule in India. Simla buzzed with activity soon after the euphoria of new found Independence had died down. Almost every building was occupied to house the large number of officers and employees shifted from Lahore. A large number of the Central Government offices were retained at Simla for want of sufficient accommodation in Delhi and some continue to remain in Simla till date.

The High Court of Punjab was located in 'Peterhoff', a former residence of the Viceroys. It, ironically, was the venue where the trial of Gandhiji's killers, was conducted. The accused were lodged in the Boileauganj lock-up and the trial was conducted in camera. The accused were later sentenced to death.

Just as thousands of Muslims had to leave Simla for the newly-formed Pakistan, an equal number of Hindu and Sikh refugees were brought to Simla for rehabilitation. That was the first and the most important job of the government and all energies were directed to settle and rehabilitate them. Since the main Punjab secretariat was shifted to Simla (though many of its offices were located in different towns of Punjab) the work of the re-settlement of refugees was coordinated at Simla. The government had also opened a large number of field offices and those reaching the camps were directed to the various towns where accommodation had been left by the Muslim migrants.

Addressing a press conference in Simla in October, 1947 the East Punjab premier, Dr. Gopi Chand Bhargava, said that his government was keen to settle the refugees and had prepared a draft scheme for their rehabilitation. He admitted that out of about 38 lakh Hindus and Sikhs evacuated from West Punjab, no less than 13 lakhs were from urban areas and belonged to middle class. According to a report published in the *Tribune*, he said that his government was "not neglectful" of the interests of the urban classes and "that these would be rehabilitated soon."

The refugees in Simla were allotted the buildings and land vacated by those who had left for Pakistan after their claims were cleared. Only a handful came back to stay in the town and that too after several months. However, for some of the migrants the travails of partition continued for several years. Among such people was also Dewan Chand Lamba for whom the pangs of partition ended only forty years later. He came to the town at the age of thirty and was given a temporary shelter in a house in Ladakhi Mohalla. He claimed a portion of that house for allotment in lieu of what he had left behind in the area under Pakistan. The government initially decided that he was not entitled to the property claimed by him and allotted the house to someone else. An endless chain of appeals, revisions, and writ petitions followed. Like many others he shuttled between Simla, Delhi, Jullundur and Ambala to seek justice. But his case lingered on for much more time than most of the other refugees. Partly due to wrong interpretation of the court orders and partly due to new problems that seemed to surface every now and then, Dewan Chand Lamba could not get justice till he was seventy. During 1986 he filed a writ petition in the Himachal Pradesh High Court seeking his right and due compensation for the agony suffered by him. The government, which found that it was cornered acted with alacrity and gave him the sale certificate soon after it received court notices. Lamba, who had lost the prime of his life in frustrating litigation was, however, not given any compensation and he was asked to withdraw his case since he had received his due property. No one could compensate him for the long and often frustrating struggle in which he spent the best part of his life.

Simla was witness to several such agonising tales though most ended in five to seven years after the independence. The greatest task before the government was to rebuild Punjab, and the erstwhile summer capital of the country occupied a backseat in the scheme of things. The Punjab Government had never thought that it would retain its capital in Simla and was looking for a more centrally located place. The committee formed by the government for a new permanent capital visited several towns including Jullundur, Amritsar and Ludhiana to study the possibility of locating the capital in either of these towns with some alterations. These towns were found to be too congested and with too little space for expansion. Since these towns had grown over the centuries, they were unplanned, and the committee pointed out that the shifting of the capital to any of these towns would involve demolition of a large number of existing buildings. These towns also lacked the basic infrastructure for sewerage and other facilities. The committee, therefore, recommended that a new site for the capital be chosen where an entirely new town could be built. The Central Government also agreed to share the expenditure on the construction of the new capital.

The committee, with its headquarters in Simla, surveyed several areas with the help of helicopters and by driving past several villages. Ultimately a tract of land, about 110 kilometres from Simla, with a backdrop of hills, and limited on either sides by two *choes* or streams, was selected. This land, west of Simla, was considered ideal. The area has now been developed into Chandigarh.

It was a strange coincidence that the planning for the new capital was done in the United Services Club where the Macmohan line was also formed and the Radcliffe line given the final shape. One of the residential blocks (now called Block IV) was converted into the office of the Capital Project and the initial plans were drawn by young Indian architects working under Albert Mayor and Maxwell Fry and later under Le Corbusier and his team of experts. Surjit Singh, who later retired as the Chief Architect of the Chandigarh Administration and then as the Chairman of the Chandigarh Housing Board, recollects that the first floor of the Block was converted into the office of the Capital Project where the plans for the new capital were prepared. Within a few years a field office was shifted to Nagla village which was to be acquired later and where Sector 27 of Chandigarh is now located.

The Punjab Government began to shift its offices to the new capital as soon as the buildings to house them were completed at Chandigarh. By 1953, the Punjab Government had formally shifted its headquarters to Chandigarh, and Simla, the summer seat of the Imperial Government and that of the Punjab Government after the Independence, went through a period of total eclipse. Hopes were revived when the Punjab Government proposed, at one time, to use it as its summer capital but the proposal never came through. Simla was relegated to the position of a distant district headquarters and while the government directed its attention for the building up of Punjab from the ashes of partition, Simla as a reminder of the Imperial rule, faced total neglect.

Its association with Himachal Pradesh, whose capital it now is, started on April 15, 1948 when the Pradesh was constituted as a Chief Commissioner's province after the merger of 31 principalities as a result of a long struggle launched by the Praja Mandal. Though Simla was not part of the province, which otherwise extended up to the fringes of Simla at Kasumpti, its first Chief Commissioner, N.C. Mehta, and his deputy E. Penderal Moon, chose Simla to be its administrative capital for lack of adequate accommodation in the areas under the new province. The Foreign Office building under the British Raj, which was later destroyed in a huge fire on May 5, 1957, was converted into the headquarters and secretariat of the province. The building was

1. The Annandale ground; a social function in progress during the British Raj period.

2. An old drawing of a fete at the Annandale ground.

3. A pencil sketch of the Mall in 1870s with the general post office building in the background. A *tonga* is seen where the present 'Scandal Point' is situated.

4. A mail *tonga* during the British period.

The Rothney Castle — residence of A.O. Hume, the founder of the Indian National Congress.

6. Lord Kitchner's residence now called 'Wild Flower Hall' — a popular tourist resort.

7.   An old picture of 'Auckland House' which was later destroyed in a fire.

8.   Simla's Walker's Hospital, now converted into Military Hospital, Simla.

9. An old view of the Geity Theatre, Simla.

10. An old view of the
Telegraph office, Simla.

12.   An old picture of Loreto Convent, Simla.

13.   *Jhampan* (Rickshaw-stand) — now largely in disuse.

14. Nehru and Jinnah at Hotel Cecil in Simla during the Simla conference.

15. Members of the Radcliff Commission at a meeting in US Club, Simla to demarcate Indo–Pakistan border.

16. Narrow gauge train from Kalka to Simla.

17. Simla ice skating rink.

19. Simla under snow.

20. Children making a snow-man
after a heavy snow-fall.

21. Shopping after a snow-fall at Simla. The life and activities continue un-hampered.

22. A scene of the Ridge under snow.

23. The Ridge — the large open and sunny spot, most sought after place by residents and visitors alike.

25. Mrs. Indira Gandhi and Mr. Zulfikar
Ali Bhutto at the Simla Summit in 1972.

26. A section of the crowd at the Ridge on February 25, 1971 where the then Prime Minister,
Mrs. Indira Gandhi formally granted statehood to Himachal Pradesh.

27. A view of the Himalayan snow-line from the Ridge.

28. A view of the Ridge; the conical building on the left was the old band-stand. It has now been converted into a restaurant.

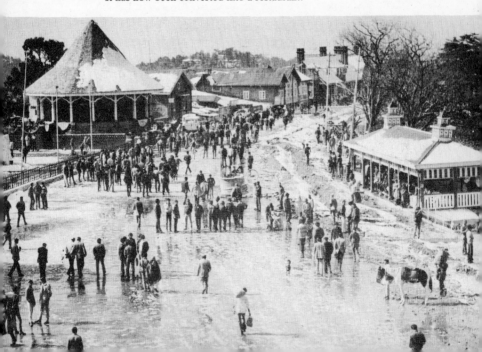

named "Himachal Dham". A little prior to the formation of the province, the then State's Minister Sardar Vallabhbhai Patel had, in a letter dated March 18, 1948, stated in reference to the formation of Himachal Pradesh that "in the final stage the area is sufficiently developed in its resources and administration, it is proposed that its constitution should be similar to that of any other province. The ultimate objective is to enable this area to attain the position of an autonomous province of India."

The long-drawn battle for "final stage" of attaining a full-fledged statehood for Himachal Pradesh was also fought from Simla by leaders like Dr. Yashwant Singh Parmar, Padam Dev, Gauri Prashad, Karam Singh, Ram Lal, Daulat Ram, Sankhyan, Lal Chand Prarthi, Hari Ram Choudhry, Mehnga Singh, Vidya Dhar, Nek Ram Negi, Satya Dev Bushehri and a host of others.

The struggle led to the enactment of part 'C' States Act, 1951 which raised the status of the Pradesh and the formation of a responsible government along with some other part 'C' States under a Lieutenant Governor. However in 1954 the States Reorganisation recommended the integration of Himachal into Punjab. This led to strong protests under the leadership of Dr. Yashwant Singh Parmar and finally in 1956 it was agreed to again convert the area into a Union Territory under a Lieutenant Governor. Again a chain of meetings of protests followed and the Himachal Territorial Council was converted into a Legislative Assembly in 1963 after the passage of the Government of Union Territories Act, 1963. Simla, as its headquarters, remained a mute witness to the evolution of Himachal Pradesh though it continued to remain a district headquarter of Punjab.

The decision to reopen the question of reorganisation of Punjab on linguistic basis was taken in 1965 and the residents of Simla, alongwith those belonging to hilly areas, took up the opportunity to demand the merger of Simla and other hill areas of Punjab with Himachal Pradesh. Their wish was granted by the Punjab Boundary Commission, which while reorganising Punjab into two separate States of Punjab and Haryana decided to integrate with Himachal Pradesh the hill districts of Kangra, Simla, Kullu and Lahaul-Spiti besides the Nalagarh area of Ambala district, parts of Una tehsil of Hoshiarpur district and parts of Pathankot tehsil in Hoshiarpur district. Thus Himachal Pradesh came to "own" Simla from November 1, 1966.

But the battle to attain a statehood for Himachal Pradesh was still not won. The Himachal leaders continued to struggle for getting it that status. The Himachal Pradesh Assembly, at a meeting in the erstwhile Council Chamber passed a resolution on January 24, 1968, stating that the "House earnestly feels that it is high time for Himachal Pradesh to be recognised as a full-fledged state and to that end, it strongly urges that the central leadership and the Union Government concede the necessary legislation without further loss of time."

The peaceful yet pursuasive agitation by the Himachal leaders led to an announcement in the Parliament on July 31, 1970 by the Prime Minister Indira Gandhi that Himachal would be granted statehood. The State of Himachal Pradesh Act was passed on December 18 of the same year and the long-standing demand of the people of the area was fulfilled.

Simla, as the capital of the new State, witnessed another important event on January 25, 1971 when the then Prime Minister Mrs. Indira Gandhi came to the historic Ridge to formally inaugurate the eighteenth State of the country. Thousands of people converged on the Ridge, which at one time was reserved only for the Viceroy's functions, and waited under a light snowfall as she drove to the Ridge to give Himachal the status of a full-fledged State.

The following year, Simla witnessed another historic event and the first such event in the independent India. It was the venue of the Indo-Pakistan summit after the 1971 war with that country. The town once again buzzed with activity and was spruced up for the big occasion. Leading the galaxy of leaders from both the countries were Indira Gandhi and Zulfikar Ali Bhutto. The attention of the entire country, as also of the world, was once again directed towards Simla for the historic conference.

The venue for the conference was spread out in various buildings, with the conspicuous exception of the Viceregal Lodge. Formal and informal meetings were held between the two delegations at the 'Ellerslie' and the 'Barnes Court' which was called the Hima-

chal Bhawan at that time and is the Governor's temporary residence now. Till the very last day, an agreement seemed to be
doubtful but at about 11.30 p.m., almost all senior delegates and
officials were directed to gather at the Himachal Bhawan and the
historic agreement was signed by the two countries to resolve their
disputes through negotiations and to end all hostilities. It was an
important landmark in the modern history of the country, and the
town of many a historical decision added another major event to
its chapter in moulding the course of history of the sub-continent.

But while the Punjab Government was busy in rebuilding
Punjab and planning to shift to its new capital and while the leaders of Himachal were waging a struggle to get it the status of a
full-fledged State, Simla itself was being totally neglected. The
facilities left by the British rulers were not improved presumably
in the belief that these were sufficient for the frugal Indian needs.
Barring the private buildings, which mushroomed in a big way, no
accommodation was added and the need to provide more housing
facilities to government employees was not realised till it was too
late. During the days when the Punjab government had its capital
in Simla, the town was able to meet their requirements and obviously the then government was not inclined to invest in its improvement since it was sure to move into its new capital at Chandigarh. Simla was therefore used only as a make-shift capital and
absolutely no heed was paid to its development. This total neglect
continued till 1966 when Simla was transferred to Himachal
Pradesh.

However, scant attention was paid to Simla even after it became the permanent, and not the rented capital of Himachal Pradesh. The need of the hour, according to the leaders at that time,
was to bring facilities in other towns in the State at par with those
in Simla. In the process, however, Simla itself began to decay and
the decline had not been arrested by the successive State Governments. One important factor for the indifferent attitude of the
governments was the fact that except for a short spell, the Simla
constituency was represented by one opposition member or the
other and consequently the desired funds were not sanctioned.
The elections to the Simla Municipal Corporation were not held
presumably out of the fear that the opposition would "capture" it.

The root cause of all the problems of Simla was the sudden spurt of population soon after the independence. The population jumped from 18,345 in 1941 to 46,150 in 1951. The British rulers had sought to restrict the population of the town mainly from the security point of view in the days of rising nationalist movement and partly because they were aware that the limited resources in Simla would not be able to hold a much larger population. The quantum jump in the population between 1941 and 1951 is also attributed to the refugees from Pakistan and the shifting of the entire paraphernalia of the Punjab Government to Simla. Several affluent residents of the adjoining areas, including the Rajas and Ranas, also decided to keep a regular establishment in Simla. The shifting of the Punjab Government offices from Simla to Chandigarh brought down the population to 42,597 according to the census taken in 1961, but it has been a story of rapid increase since its merger in Himachal Pradesh in 1966 and its ultimate emergence as the permanent capital of the State. Thus, according to the 1971 census, the population of the town increased by nearly 30 per cent to 55,326. The population swelled to nearly 75,000 during 1981 and is now estimated to be in the vicinity of one lakh. This is supplemented by a large number of tourists to the town and the residents of Himachal Pradesh in connection with government work and court cases. Thus while the permanent population of Simla has shot up by 400 per cent, its basic infrastructure of facilities has remained more or less static since the independence. The few developmental activities seem negligible in view of the population boom and the facilities left by the British are being used, as it were, with a vengeance.

The increased population led to an unbearable strain on the civic amenities. Almost every patch of land in the town was sold and purchased and the new constructions completed clogged the town. While the government remained busy with issues of public importance, the people threw all rules to wind and the officials preferred to compound the cases after imposing minor fines. The town not only grew congested but high-rising concrete monsters raised heads in the most sought-after areas in the town. The effort of the British rulers, to make Simla the "most British" town and their insistence on the retention of hill architecture, had no meaning for the people, nor for the officials administering the town.

They even did not bother for the fact that the town is located in a highly seismic area and unplanned growth could lead to great dangers in the future.

Though under the existing rules, the felling of trees was prohibited in Simla but permission to fell trees to construct houses and commercial buildings was granted for the asking. Nature was completely disregarded and it led to a serious problem. Instead of reducing the loads from top of slopes, the excavated material was dumped and more loads were imposed through heavy constructions which caused instability of slopes. The result was "creep movements", as the geologists put it, or sinking of some parts of Simla.

The first sinking was reported in 1942 in the Lakkar Bazar area. The street was reported to have settled down by several feet, and the entire foundation of a big building nearby was reinforced by supporting it on R.C.C. piers resting directly on the rock. In the subsequent years, and particularly after 1956, creeping movement or sinking of land was reported from several parts of the town. Localised damage to slopes was also reported from near 'Barnes Court' or Himachal Bhawan, 'Rockery', 'Rooknest' and the Summer Hill. However, the cracks and sinking of area were more noticeable and more dangerous around the Ridge. At the time of the construction of the water tank under the Ridge and its subsequent extension following a fire in which several shops were gutted when it was decided to provide alternative sites to the shopkeepers and to extend the area, the soil excavated from the tank was dumped to level and extend the Ridge. The bitumen coating over the Ridge and above the water tank is two feet thick and no damage was caused to it but the slides and cracks in the adjoining area, particularly towards the Lakkar Bazar, during 1965, 1971 and 1974 caused panic among the residents of Simla. The damage during 1971 was extensive. Several buildings developed cracks and parts of Lakkar Bazar road sank. The 'Bayneston', the D.A.V. School, the old and the new Labour Hostels in the area suffered heavy damage.

The Central Building Research Institute (CBRI) was requested to investigate the causes for the damage and to suggest remedial measures. The team of experts submitted a comprehensive plan and pointed out that the lack of proper drainage facilities, the lack of vegetation and the growth of technically ill-planned buildings in the area were responsible for the damage.

Unfortunately little heed was paid to the recommendations, and the sinking, though on a lesser scale, is reported almost every year. As late as in January 1987, after a spell of snowfall, fresh cracks were reported on the Lakkar Bazar road. The local administration, to top it all, announced the construction of a major commercial centre near the area most affected by the sinking. The foundation stone of the complex was hastily laid but a public outcry halted the construction of the complex. Fresh surveys were carried out and it was stated that the area falls under a 'loose-zone'. It was recommended that the foundation of the proposed building should rest on hard rocks rather than on loose soil as initially planned. Even during 1976 the Central Road Research Institute was asked to conduct a survey. The Institute, in its report (which for unknown reasons was marked confidential) had attributed the reasons of damage to "the en masse movement in the mantle of slopes." It pointed out that the sound bed-rock had not been affected but "the other factors responsible for the slope failure were the inadequate design of the walls, movement of heavily-loaded trucks on roads which cause damage to the underground water pipes, frost action increase in overburden due to excavation of loose fill and loss of fine material in the subsoil due to seepage of water."

The Institute, in its report, stressed the need for construction of additional retaining structures and strengthening of the existing retaining walls and breast walls along the Ridge. The retaining wall of the Ridge towards the north is about 6.8 metres high and 55 metres in length, which, according to the report, was built on the "partially consolidated fill to widen the Ridge area."

The recommendations of the experts, unfortunately, have largely remained ignored. Some half-hearted attempts were made but the experts are of the opinion that concerted action is called for. The absence of vegetation and the huge pressure on the drainage system are among the reasons cited for taking immediate steps to avoid any catastrophe.

The decay of Simla is reflected in the functioning of the Municipal Corporation after independence. Till the town was merged with Punjab and even much after that, the Municipality had remained in the charge of junior officials. They were posted only to mark time before a better posting. The result was that, for one, their tenure was too short and secondly they had no roots in the town. The public representation to the organisation (since its conversion into a Corporation) came only after 25 years following a struggle waged by certain public-spirited residents who filed a writ petition in the public interest. The High Court of the Himachal Pradesh gave the verdict in their favour. The government went in appeal before the Surpreme Court but it was directed to hold the elections within a time schedule. As it happened the results of the first election in 1986 caused more confusion. The Mayor belonging to the Congress (I) does not enjoy a majority support and the functioning of the Corporation has come to a grinding halt. Squabbles between the members, on such incredible issues as the placement of garbage cans, have reduced the functioning of the Corporation to mockery.

Gone are the days when it wielded great power and importance. It was first constituted in 1852 according to the Government of India notification of December 15, 1851. In view of the pressure from the house-owners, a new constitution of the Committee, as it was then called, was framed in 1855. It was then composed of all elected members and only the Deputy Commissioner was its *ex-officio* member. However, three more *ex-officio* members were nominated to it in 1864. During 1871 it was given the status of a first class Municipality. Between 1876 and 1883, the strength of the Committee was reduced to five nominated members, two house-owners and two salaried officials after A.O. Hume and some other house-owners in Simla launched an attack on the "despotic and arbitrary tendencies" of the Municipality. A Committee was formed to enquire about the desirability of having an elected Municipality. The Committee, by a majority decision, recommended a wholly-elected Municipal Committee though Hume favoured a gradual process towards that aim. The elections to the Municipality were held in 1883 and several new schemes were initiated but the Municipality had remained in debt since 1877. The elections to the Municipality were held on the basis of property owned by individuals in Simla. Following a rapid increase in the government buildings, particularly during 1880s, the government claimed more representation and nominated members from its quota. This led to a sharp decrease in the interest shown by individuals. Following fresh agitation, the constitution of the Committee was suspended in 1890 and a new Committee was formed in 1891 with four nominated and six elected members.

Subsequently during 1900, the elected seats were reduced to five and again in 1907 it was reconstituted with just seven members. Its fortunes never looked up and it remained dominated by the government officials since then. The nominations were also made on pick and choose basis but it continued to play a vital role and managed a large number of services. These included electricity, water, public health, education, medical, public works, markets and transportation system.

Simla was at that time the highest taxed town in the country. The taxes per head in 1890 were calculated at Rs. 7 and 8 Annas per head while during the same period the average tax burden in Calcutta was Rs. 6 and 6 Annas per head and in Bombay it was Rs. 6 and 12 Annas per head. During the same period the tax per head in most Punjab towns was roughly Re. one. The average income of the Municipality during 1893-1903 was Rs. 4.2 lakhs while its expenditure was Rs. 4.1 lakhs during the same period.

In a letter to the Editor of the *Pioneer*, published on August 3, 1881, A.O. Hume had regretted:

"Simla is already one of the most heavily taxed spots in the Empire, and further taxation is being proposed. The Municipality is heavily in debt. Nevertheless this Municipality is about to borrow two lakhs or more rupees to build a kursaal; as I am informed, a place of amusement, practically for the upper ten thousand (or rather *here* five hundred) only. To me this seems indefensible. I know I shall be *told* that the thing will *pay*, but more than 30 years' experience in India makes me *certain* that if this kursaal continues the property of the Municipality, it will

not pay. It is, it seems to me, somewhat of an abuse of power
to devote two lakhs of rupees raised, as in the long run
it must be, by taxation of the native and middle class
Eurasian and European population, to the provision of a
place of amusement for the higher and wealthier class. But
while this Municipality can borrow Rs. two lakhs to build
a kursaal for the 5 per cent of wealthy folks, they cannot
afford Rs. one lakh to provide a decent hospital urgently
required for the entire population. At present there is no
place to which a sick or wounded European or Eurasian
can be taken, and only accommodation for eighteen beds
for natives in the miserable cramped dispensary which does
duty for a hospital at Simla, now officialy accepted as the
summer capital of the Empire. . . ."

The annual receipts of the Corporation during 1985-86 totalled Rs. 1.71 crores while its expenditure was Rs. 1.72 crores exclu-
ding the huge grants-in-aid given by the government. The grants-
in-aid under different 'heads' totalled Rs. 57 lakhs for specific
projects. A large amount of the grants could not be used because
these are tagged to clearance of projects which more often take
unduly long periods. The salary and establishment bill of the
Corporation during the same period was a monumental Rs. 1.25
crores which left hardly any amount worth the name for developmental purposes. There has been a sharp increase in the number
of regular and temporary employees from about 300 in 1955 to
about 1250 now.

This increase is in sharp contrast to the draining of the resources of the Corporation over the years. Most of its important
functions and sources of revenue were taken over by the government beginning with the motor transportation system, the medical
institutions and the schools and colleges. Its electricity department, which was a good source of income was handed over to the
State Electricity Board in the early 70s. Its most important source
of revenue was the collection of octroi. It was abolished in 1981
and instead the government announced that it would give grant
each year in lieu of the income from octroi. However, the grant
has been much less and provides for an escalation of just seven

per cent per year. Thus during 1986 alone, the loss to the Corporation from the abolition of octroi was worth several lakhs of rupees.

Its finances are in such a bad shape that it finds it difficult even to pay the wage bill of the employees. It is supposed to pay for the street-lighting to the Electricity Board but is unable to pay and consequently its accumulated debt to the Board is nearly Rs. 1.2 crores. Since it does not have the capacity to pay for the water supplies by the Irrigation and Public Health Department, the government itself has paid Rs. 97 lakhs to the department for water supply on behalf of the Corporation. Under the existing rules, the tax on buildings cannot be raised until these are sold and repurchased. Thus the Corporation is getting a negligible amount of taxes as most of the transactions do not give the actual amount involved. For instance, the present cost of a building could entail the Corporation to get a tax of say Rs. 1,000, but it is actually getting a mere sum of Rs. 10 or so.

The Corporation, as constituted in its present shape by the Himachal Pradesh Municipal Corporation Act, 1978, has left several areas undefined. This has not only resulted in overlapping but also passing of the buck to the District administration and a host of other agencies like the Simla Development Authority and the Housing Board. An official report on the "activities and programmes" in Simla district 1982-83 pointed out that the problems of Simla are different from other towns because it is also a State Capital. "No mechanism of coordination between the District administration and Municipal Corporation, Simla has been provided, with the result that the District administration is a silent spectator to various problems of the town." The report said that the services of the Deputy Commissioner, the Superintendent of Police and other district officials are not utilised by the Corporation and "many provisions of the act are defunct and create more problems than solving them." It suggested, that it is "high-time" when a fresh look should be given to the Municipal Corporation Act to provide for effective coordination at the district level.

For lack of clear-cut rules several powers have been appropriated by the Deputy Commissioner of the district and in several projects, it has led to overlapping. Even the revenue and building records of the Corporation have been entirely handed over to the District administration. The erosion of the power of the Corporation can be substantiated by the fact that though every building constructed in the Municipal area must have a prior approval from the Corporation, the rule is followed by other government organisations more in its breach. The construction of a fast-food counter on the Ridge and some additional buildings in the complex of the Deputy Commissioner's office were taken up without the approval of the Municipal Corporation or the Town and Country Planning Department. The Corporation itself followed the same path, when in late 1986, it decided to construct 18 shops under the Mall road—the notice of the Town and Country Planning Department and the Simla Development Authority notwithstanding.

It is ironic that the water supply system erected by the British about a hundred years ago is still the main source of water supply in the town while the population of the town has risen four-fold. Augmentation schemes to provide more water were carried out in recent years and that too were far from satisfactory and much below the standard demand. An official audit report pointed out that the thickness of the pipes laid from Gumma to Simla during 1981-82 was only five to seven mm as against the required thickness of 12.5 mm. Hydraulic tests on the newly laid pipes revealed leakage at no less than 35 points from hairline cracks. The newly installed motor got burnt down almost immediately and lakhs of rupees have been spent on its repair. On the other hand, the 100-year old pumping set, said to be the oldest and largest in Asia, has been giving a sufficiently good service. The time has, of course, taken its toll and the leakage from pipes laid about a 100 years ago has assumed serious proportion. According to official sources more than 35 per cent of the water supply from the pumping stations is lost due to leakage from worn-out pipes.

Partly due to the heavy leakage and partly due to the large population, the water supply system in the town is in doldrums. Recently, the Corporation faced heavy weather in view of strong criticism from the Press for the supply of contaminated and inadequate water. The authorities pointed out that the 100-year old system required a thorough change and all the old pipes are required to be replaced. But it would require a huge amount of funds which the Corporation does not have and which the government has not been willing to provide. A proposal to strengthen the system at a cost of Rs. 55 lakhs is lying in the cold storage. Another scheme to augment the Simla water supply, costing about Rs. 35 crores, has been prepared. Ironically, Major General Beresford had suggested the same scheme about a hundred years ago. He had recommended that the water from Sutlej river be lifted to Simla to meet its growing need for water. The British government had rejected his suggestion and had pointed out that it would involve (at that time) an expenditure of about Rs. 25 lakhs. Instead it was proposed to tap water from natural springs and streams and to extend the catchment area of the reservoir. Since neither the Corporation has the money nor the State Government can afford the amount, it has been decided to approach the Central Government to provide the funds. How long will it take the Central Government to clear the funds and execute the work is anybody's guess.

It is also interesting to note that practically no improvement has been made on sewerage system in the town since 1893. The system has certainly been extended to some areas which were not connected but the main town has the same sewerage lines, which, like the water pipelines, have outlived their life. Frequent leaks are noticed causing insanitation and unhygienic conditions. The inadequate number of public lavatories are also kept unclean and the Corporation has come in for severe criticism but it has made no impact.

The natural drains and *nullahs*, which the British had so scrupulously tried to keep clean, have clogged and have become a favourite dumping ground. During the spurt of building activity in the town, the waste or unused building material was also dumped in the *nullahs* which have caused insanitation and the slush water generally gets spilled out causing damage to nearby buildings. The officials claim that there has been a substantial increase in the number of safai mazdoors and admit that their workload has decreased, but the sanitary conditions in the town are worse than ever. With security of service guaranteed and political backing, the safai mazdoors now constitute a formidable force and the Corporation cannot take any harsh decisions against them. On the three occasions in the recent years, the Corporation had to taste their wrath. During their strike in 1976, 1980 and again in 1986, the Corporation watched helplessly as they struck work for periods ranging from a week to a fortnight and put the Simla water and sewerage system out of gear. At one time the Corporation had to seek the help of the armed forces to keep the water flowing. Their agitations for more facilities or against the "insult" meted out to one of their members, has become a regular feature and the vantage point of the Municipal office gives them ample opportunity to attract public attention.

Partly due to political reasons, the Corporation is unable to use several powers vested in it. During the Raj days, the house-owners were required to paint the roofs of their houses at least once in two years. At the expiry of the period, the Corporation used to get the paint done and charge a penalty besides the cost of painting from the house-owners. The Corporation still has that power but does not use it. During the emergency era, the Corporation had acted and the town was given a face-lift. The residents were advised to get the roofs of their houses painted and those who defaulted had to pay a heavy penalty after the task was completed by the Corporation. The town now gives a shanty look and even the government buildings look ill-maintained and dilapidated. In 1982, a high-powered Committee of the government decided that a plan for the face-lifting of the town should be given priority. It was proposed that the plan would include removal of dirt from outside the buildings, painting of roofs and windows, repair of downpipes and repair of roofs. The official report on Simla during 1982-83 noted that "it was also decided (by the Committee) that after a plan of improvement for each building has been made by the Municipal Corporation, some assistance could be provided by Deputy Commissioner who could distribute this work in each area to the Magistrates" and who would persuade the people to undertake the improvement. However, it noted that "unfortunately nothing tangible has been done in this direction. The Municipal Corporation has sufficient legal authority to enforce this type of improvement. . . ."

The large number of unclaimed or disputed houses left by the Muslims who shifted at the time of partition, were handed over to the Waqf Board. Since the Waqf Board is not a private organisation, it has made no effort to get the tenants evicted or made them to pay higher rents. Consequently, the rents fixed in the initial period after the partition, have not been changed and are incredibly low. The tenants do not like to spend money on repair or renovation of these houses since they are not the owners. The Board, which gets a pathetically low income, is in no position to improve the conditions of the houses. With the result that almost all of these houses are in dilapidated condition.

The government must also share responsibility for the ramshackle look of the town. While the leaders often urge the residents to improve and renovate their houses, the condition of government-owned buildings is not much better. The 1982-83 official report on Simla District pointed out that "when we ask the private owners to improve their buildings and paint them, it will be necessary for the government to improve its buildings. This may require extra funds by the Public Works Department but for the face-lifting of Simla, this is an inevitable expense." The funds have not been sanctioned till date.

Not that schemes for the improvement or face-lifting of the town were not prepared in the previous years. In fact there were an impressive array of schemes which of course, never saw the light of the day. As early as 1971, a thick booklet was printed to spell out no less than 22 high-sounding schemes. It is interesting to note that 15 years later only four of these schemes have become a reality. According to the Master Plan then drawn, the town was to have an aerial ropeway, additional lifts, new bus terminus, a huge auditorium, a holiday home, multi-storied parking facilities, rest houses, and several other projects.

Again during the early part of the 1980s, fresh plans were drawn, which were called Interim Development Plans. The town was divided into seven zones "to arrest the decay and haphazard growth" of the town and to diversify its growth by creating suburbs. An official spokesman described the Plan to be "designed to satisfy immediate needs and to meet long-term objectives within the aims of economically viable, socially satisfying and aesthetically inspiring project." Subsequently, the State Planning Authority prepared a Master Plan with a projected population of 3.17 lakhs during 2001. According to the land-use map of the Simla Master Plan, 48.77 per cent of the total land is proposed to be used for residential purposes, 2.5 per cent for industries, 8.75 per cent for public facilities, 16.28 per cent for recreation, 8.95 per cent for roads and footpaths and an area of 3856 acres is proposed to be left untouched. Three-fourths of the total area is proposed to be retained as a "green belt" and the plan also includes the development of an artificial lake.

The latest plan is estimated to cost Rs. 125 crores and the State Government is banking on the Central Government to finance the project. It has to be cleared by several Central Government agencies but, according to the authorities, it has got preliminary sanction.

The steep rise in the population and the consequent growth in the number of vehicles and their movements has led to a serious traffic problem in the town. The Cart Road, which was not initially designed for heavy vehicles, is being put to use for all types of heavy vehicles while the width of the road around the town has been widened only marginally. The result is frequent traffic jams on the road. A bye-pass for trucks and other goods carriers is under construction. Alongwith the problem of traffic congestion is the problem of inadequate parking places. This forces a large number of motorists to park their vehicles on the main road. A number of plans to provide parking lots have remained on paper.

The congestion in the Lower Bazar area, which had been described by Rudyard Kipling so vividly, has been compounded with the steep increase in the population. Squatters and shopkeepers have clogged the bazar and it was again on the intervention of the High Court that the road was cleared some years ago. It is now almost back to square one. Encroachments have become a part of Simla life, and the Municipality, more often, likes to turn a blind eye.

One of the greatest problems faced by the employees and new-comers to the town is the acute shortage of accommodation for which the British had so studiously made plans. All restrictions were obviously lifted after independence on people coming and settling in the town and its population swelled beyond its capacity. Not that the houses were not constructed. In fact, the number of houses constructed in Simla after the independence is about three times more than what the former rulers had been able to construct during their stay of over a hundred years. Almost every available space has been filled up with "ugly buildings" without caring for any rules or regulations. However, the increase in the building activity was not in proportion to the increase in population and the government paid absolutely no heed to increase government accommodation.

The result is that over 80 per cent of the employees in Simla are now staying in rented accommodation and only the lucky few, a majority of whom are officers, get the government accommodation. Barring a few houses, which proved to be merely drop in the ocean, no government residential scheme was prepared. The great demand for residential accommodation obviously led to rents skyrocketing and, according to a preliminary survey, most employees residing in private rented accommodation, are spending nearly 50 per cent of their salary towards the rents. One of the factors for the quantum jump in the rents is also attributed to employees of banks or private organisations who are paid substantial house rent allowance by their respective companies and therefore can afford to pay heavy rents. The worst sufferers are the junior government employees.

Far from constructing office accommodation, the government and its various Corporations and Boards have actually established their offices in private residential buildings which has contributed to the shortage of residential accommodation and increase in rents. The Imperial rulers had strictly forbidden establishment of offices in residential areas. The public sector undertakings like the banks and other established organisations pay heavy rents and the tenants prefer to accommodate them rather than individual tenants. Some of the offices are deliberately located in private buildings owned by senior officers and are paid huge rents to "please" them.

6

A Tourist Town

It was the seat of power during the British Raj at its peak and is now the capital of a fledgling peaceful and beautiful state. Yet it is known better as a summer resort and a tourist town. It is preferred by the tourists more for its scenic beauty and to escape, even though for a short period, from the oppressive heat of the plains during summers. It is publicised, and is thus more famous, for its snow-fall when the entire town is covered under a thick blanket of snow and when it looks like a dream town. Being one of the few tourist towns in the country which receives snow-fall and which is easily accessible, people flock to it during the peak winter period to experience the joy of snow-fall. A majority of them camp for days together in the town and some have to leave disappointed if the weather gods decide to keep the sky clear. Then there are numerous tourists who prefer to visit the town during the mystic monsoon when the low-hanging clouds and thick fog reduces visibility to merely a few feet. Again, some others get enchanted with its beauty during the spring season when multicoloured flowers bloom in the ever-green surroundings. The town is publicised for "all reasons, for all seasons" and, ironically, not for its place in the history. The glossy publicity brochures refer to its past in the passing and there is no reference to the several majestic buildings and historic sites with which is associated the British Raj and our freedom struggle.

Yet no visitor to the town can miss the thought of its history and its British connection. In his *Bound to Exile*, Michael Edwards had written: "The whole town gave the impression of having been transported from Surrey in a badly packed parcel and accidently dropped in Tibet". That was a century ago. It is not the scene in the present times but its skyline is a strong reminder of the by-gone era. Along with the historic Viceregal Lodge, the imposing Christ Church and several other old and magnificent buildings of the yore, are the new constructions like the university campus, the new secretariat building and numerous conspicuous concrete structures besides temples, gurdwaras and mosques.

Now it is neither a British town, nor an old Indian town—it is a synthesis of the both. One critic has described it as a show-window of the worst form of Victorian and modern architecture. Being the only town of its size which was exclusively developed for British residents, it is not dominated by any particular community—no, not even the local Himachalis. It has a fair sprinkling of Punjabis, the Soods, the Kashmiris and, of course, the Himachalis. On the whole, the town has acquired a metropolitan character and a majority of its residents are employees of the State Government, the Central Government and private enterprises. The town is inundated by various hues of tourists particularly during the summers. It is believed, though never quite properly surveyed, that during the peak tourist season, the number of tourists outnumber the local population of the town.

Simla has acquired its present status as a tourist town not because of any design on the part of the administrators who were at the helm of its affairs. In fact no effort whatsoever was made to project the town as a tourist destination till the town was merged with Himachal Pradesh. It is only in the recent years that the State Government has realised the immense tourist potential of the town and the extent of economy it can generate. A State Tourism Development Corporation (better known as the HPTDC) has been created and is engaged in the promotion of tourism in the entire State including the Simla circuit with all the places of tourist attraction in and around Simla. The efforts of the State Government have already begun to pay dividends which is reflected in the increasing number of tourists who visit the town and the State every year.

The Corporation regularly publicises the places of tourist attraction and has also opened tourist information offices in big cities like Delhi, Bombay and Madras besides at two strategic locations in Simla itself. Tourist literature, brochures, guide maps, posters and picture postcards are available at these offices. It runs conducted sight-seeing tours during the tourist season. Special tours are arranged by it for groups or on sufficient demand from the tourists. It has accommodation for tourists at Simla and at some strategic locales in the suburbs. The tourist information offices of the HPTDC also make reservations for various hotels and lodges managed by it.

The efforts notwithstanding, not enough has still been done to project Simla's relics of the past, and the steps taken to develop tourism in the town have been inadequate. On its part, the State Government has declared tourism as an industry and has formulated schemes to help private entrepreneurs who might like to develop tourist complexes and hotels. Indeed a large number of them have benefited from the various schemes including subsidies and loans. Over 125 registered hotels and about 40 unregistered hotels have sprung up in the town during the last few years. The tourism department of the State Government is supposed to fix the tariff of the registered hotels and ensure its implementation. However, the orders are generally violated during the peak rush periods due to acute pressure on accommodation. The repeated assertion of the government, that stricter enforcement of the rules would be undertaken, has not had the desired result in the recent years.

The government has also not been able to create any place of tourist interests like recreation centres, gardens, children parks or amusement centres. Not enough attention has been paid to improve public conveniences, and special steps are not taken for cleanliness of the town even during the heavy rush of the tourists. The government also exercises no control over the taxi operators who misguide and fleece the tourists. The porters too get inclined to fleece the unwary tourists.

One of the major problems faced by the tourists in Simla is the lack of guides and conducted tours within the town. Thus very few tourists to the town are able to visit places like the

Viceregal Lodge which has been renamed as Rashtrapati Niwas and now houses the Indian Institute of Advanced Study. Despite repeated demands, this magnificent building has not been converted into museum or art gallery. The Institute does not allow tourists to visit the premises except during specified periods each evening. The Viceroy's office is now occupied by the director of the Institute and not open for the tourists. The historic conference hall is usually converted into dining hall during seminars and meetings. Most visitors return little wiser because there is no one to explain them the importance of the building and its various annexes.

Similarly, the Imperial Government's secretariat now houses the offices of the Accountant-General and is not open for tourists. The Railway Board building, which has a unique architecture to absorb earthquake shocks, is now occupied by numerous Central Government offices. The 'Barnes Court', which served as the residence of Commanders-in-Chief of the Imperial army and lieutenant-governors of erstwhile Punjab, is now the temporary residence of the Governor of Himachal Pradesh. He would shift to a new building which is under construction at the site of the 'Peterhoff' which was gutted in a devastating fire in the early eighties. The 'Barnes Court' would then revert back to its role as the State guest house.

The 'Rothney Castle', one-time residence of the founder of the Indian National Congress, Mr. A.O. Hume, is being converted into an exclusive luxury hotel. It was from this house that Hume had initiated correspondence with various organisations and individuals and had conceived the formation of the Congress. Despite a strong public outcry, and ironically during the very centenary year of the Congress, the house was partly dismantled to make way for the luxurious hotel. The proprietors have decided to leave intact a room or two as tourist attraction. The Castle is located on way to the Jakhu Temple and provides a magnificent view of the Simla hills. A stone plaque and an old ramshackled *jhampanee* in the courtyard of the house are the only reminders of its past.

The Jakhu temple itself is one of the most favoured spots for the tourists to Simla. The Hanuman temple, which provided the nucleus for the present town, is located about three kilometres from the Ridge. According to mythology, Hanuman stopped at the site of the temple on his way back after collecting the *sanjeevani booti* for Lakshmana. Apart from the religious beliefs and the reverence the Hindus have for the temple, it provides a nice experience to the tourists. The approach to the temple is through a dense forest of deodars though many tourists find the steep climb tiresome. Ponies are also available for the journey to and back from the temple. Being located at the highest point in the town, the temple overlooks a breathtaking view of the valley on all sides.

The Ridge and the Mall road remain the favourite spots with the tourists and the residents alike. However, few tourists treading on the historic Ridge realise that they are walking over a large water reservoir which supplies water to the town. The century-old reservoir is covered with a thick coat of tarcoal, sand and concrete. The Ridge was the site of official functions during the British rule and is still reserved for all official functions. An octagonal structure which was the band-stand, has now been converted into a restaurant managed by the HPTDC. Since the Ridge is the only place in the town which provides some relief from the undulating hilly terrain, many people prefer to relax and walk over the Ridge. It also gets a full compliment of sun-shine unlike other areas in the town. It is a paradise for children because of the near absence of traffic. The added attraction for them are the pony rides and the softy ice-cream counters. The Mall, which joins the road from the Ridge at the 'scandal point' (named so because it was the favourite place for gossip mongers during the British rule), is reputed to be the place in Simla where you can meet almost everyone in the town during the evenings. It is a busy shopping centre and gives the look of a colourful fair during the summer months.

The famous Gaiety theatre, the birthplace of amateur theatre in India, is located right along the Mall. It was patronised by Viceroys, Generals and theatre-lovers but now seems to have fallen on bad days. It is but rarely that plays are staged in the theatre but the interior of the theatre has been preserved and deserves a look. The government plans to renovate the theatre in the near future.

Besides 'Malling' (a word coined by the local people to describe the favourite pastime of some residents to walk up and down the Mall road), the town and its surroundings offer a number of walks which are both delightful and pleasant. The State Government has declared a stretch of the Mall road as "sealed". No vehicle barring those of the fire brigade or ambulance and, rarely those belonging to VIPs, are allowed in the "sealed" portion. Some other roads have been declared as 'restricted' and one has to seek prior permission to ply a vehicle on such roads. These restrictions are indeed welcome for the pedestrians.

While the Mall road generally remains crowded and busy, one can take the Forest road for a quieter walk. It branches off from the Ridge and involves a gentle climb. After running parallel to the Mall road, though at a higher elevation, it joins the national highway near Sanjauli beyond Chhota Simla. Some residents prefer to call it "Lovers' lane". However, the original 'Lovers' lane' is now a busy road and is used by heavy vehicles to encircle the Simla hill for a one-way traffic. It breaks off from the Victory tunnel and after winding its way along the ice skating rink and 'Auckland House', it emerges at Sanjauli to join the main road.

Another road, which also joins the Ridge with Sanjauli, cuts across the Lakkar Bazar. The scene from the road, which is not exactly a pedestrian's paradise, is excellent. One can view the snow-clad Himalayan ranges from the 'other side' of Simla. It is about three kilometres in length.

Towards the west of the town there is an interesting walk involving a distance of about four kilometres to a picnic spot called the 'Glen'. The small, beautiful valley has a narrow stream and is a good site for excursions and picnic. The path to the Glen takes off from near the Chaura Maidan and winds its way through a dense growth of deodars and pines. The main road from Chaura Maidan to the Summer Hill, the seat of the Himachal Pradesh University, provides an interesting and varied scenery and is frequently used by university students and staff. Summer Hill is about six kilometres from the heart of the town and provides an enchanting view of Simla.

Certain hill-tops in the suburbs of Simla provide a breath-taking view of the surroundings. One such spot is the Prospect Hill near Boileauganj which is located on way to Taradevi. A small temple at the top of the hill is dedicated to the Kamana Devi. Yet another hill-top worth an excursion, and for a different scenic beauty, is Tara Devi itself. The hill-top is about nine kilo-metres from the town but one can also take a short train or bus ride upto Taradevi township before the climb to the top.

One of the most popular walks around Simla is located to-wards the north-east of the town. It takes off from the tourist resort of Wild Flower Hall and culminates at Kufri. It is an enchanting short walk and the path winds its way through deodar, oak and pine trees. There are, of course, many number of small paths and lanes in the neighbourhood of Simla which can be ex-plored by the visitors and tourists. The people are generally co-operative and pleasant. The best period for excursions and walks is from March to June and from September to November.

The same period is also considered ideal for longer treks in the region. Simla is emerging as a good base for such trekking in the mid-Himalayan ranges. One of the longer trekking routes, which is gaining immense popularity, emanates from Sarahan near Ram-pur in Simla district. It involves a walk of seven days to Aut which is located between Kulu and Manali. The trek is via Rampur, across the Jalori Pass, Shoja and Larji. About half a dozen treks, involving four to fifteen days, emanate from Kulu-Manali region. The Himachal Pradesh Tourism Development Corporation organi-ses partly conducted trekking tours each year. These have become very popular but are restricted because of the limited accommo-dation available through the routes.

There are certain other places in the town which are worth a visit but not many tourists are even aware of them because of a lack of proper guidance. The Himachal Pradesh State Museum near Chaura Maidan has several delightful and historically im-portant items. It has a rich collection of Kangra paintings, ancient idols, coins, costumes and other artefacts. The State Government has also recently opened a State Archives. It is located a little farther from the High Court complex and can be of great interest

to the tourists who love antiquity. It has several invaluable historical documents and records.

About ten kilometres from the heart of the town is the Tuti-
kandi zoo. However, the road to the zoo is in a bad condition and
fit only for the plying of jeeps. The chief attractions at the zoo
are wolf cubs reared in captivity and the State bird 'The Monal'.
Most tourists find it tedious to visit the zoo and return disappointed. There is a plan to shift the zoo at a more convenient location. The tourist literature also includes the tempting 'Chad-
wik falls' but it turns out to be most disappointing because there
is nothing but a small seasonal water-fall at the site. The Annandale
ground, which was the favourite site for fun and frivolity, picnics
and fairs during the Raj days, is a training ground for army per-
sonnel. The Durand Cup football tournament was started from
this ground but no sport competition takes place at this ground
now. It is also used as a helipad.

Nearly 60 kilometres from Simla is a place called 'Tattapani'
which literally means hot water. It is a hot water sulphur spring
but has not yet been fully developed which leads to acute dis-
appointment. The spring, unlike at other places, does not flow
over-ground and one has to remove sand at particular spots to
discover the hot water. There are proposals to develop it and to
construct bathing areas. A forest rest house is located near the
springs but it does not have catering facilities. It is proposed to
construct a cafe and rest house and with the passage of time, the
spot may turn out to be another centre of tourist attraction.

On way to Tattapani, roughly half-way from Simla, is a beautiful nine-hole golf course at Naldera. It is considered to be a
unique undulating golf-course, believed to be the highest of its
kind, where the British officers escaped to avoid the "tyranny of
the dreaded despatch boxes." It is well-maintained and is an ideal
picnic spot. The HPTDC maintains a good tourist bungalow and
log-huts which are comfortable and cosy. Enroute to Naldera are
several scenic spots including the 'Retreat' and the Craignano,
which are being maintained as State guest houses. Mashobra,
another scenic place is also located on way to Naldera.

Kufri, 15 kilometres from Simla, provides a breathtaking
view of the snow-clad mountain ranges in the distance and lush

green valleys around it. Kufri was once more famous for skiing but since the snow-line has shifted northward, it has yielded place to Narkanda for the winter sport. For amateurs, however, Kufri still retains the charm and a large number of tourists visit the area during winters. Besides a small tourist lodge of the HPTDC, the place has recently acquired a magnificent private tourist complex. A small zoo at the '*Chini* Bungalow' and yak ride makes it a delightful visit to Kufri. Just about ten kilometres away is a place called Fagu which has one of the most beautifully located tourist bungalows. It is located on a ridge and provides a panoramic view.

On the same route, about 13 kilometres from Simla, is another complex called the Wild Flower Hall. The majestic old building, which has now been converted into a hotel and restaurant, is another delightful place for the tourists. Its well-maintained lawns and gardens are a visual treat. A memorable short trek to Kufri also takes off from the Wild Flower Hall. The accommodation at the complex remains heavily booked during the tourist seasons. About fifty kilometres away from the Wild Flower Hall is Narkanda which is fast developing into a popular winter resort for its fine skiing slopes. The HPTDC runs short duration coaching courses in skiing for amateurs and enthusiasts. It also has a tourist bungalow for the tourists. Located at an elevation of about 9000 feet, the place is colder than Simla.

Chail, one of the loveliest resorts in the region, is located about 45 kilometres from Simla via Kufri. It was the summer capital of the erstwhile State of Patiala. The palaces and guest houses of the former rulers have been converted into various hotels and lodges by the HPTDC and are well-maintained. Chail is ideal for a quite holiday. It also boasts of the highest cricket pitch in the world which is now the playground for the students of Military School located there. Chail affords a magnificent view of Simla which is particularly bewitching at night. To avoid a repetition of the route, one could go back to Kalka via Kandaghat which is about 30 kilometres from Chail on the national highway.

A number of tourist lodges and rest houses have been created by the HPTDC along the route from Kalka to Simla. These include a snack-bar and tourist lodge at Parwanu, a sprawling tourist complex at Barog, a tourist bungalow at Solan and a small rest house and restaurant at Kiarighat.

Simla is well-connected by road, rail and air services. Luxury and ordinary buses leave Delhi (360 kilometres) and Chandigarh (115 kilometres) every half an hour. The total journey time from Delhi to Simla is about nine hours, and about four hours from Chandigarh to Simla. Taxies are also available on hire from Kalka for the hill region of the State. Special luxury buses are pressed into service during the tourist season.

The town is connected by the century-old narrow gauge "toy-train". It is a memorable experience to ride the train to Simla from Kalka although it takes a little more time to cover the distance. There are two connecting trains to Simla from Delhi and one from Amritsar and Jammu. Concessional tickets are available for the tourists.

The town was connected by air services only in 1987. It has a comparatively small airstrip at Jubbar-hatti, about 30 kilometres from the heart of the town. The Vayudoot has introduced a daily flight from Delhi via Chandigarh. The same flight connects Simla with the Kulu valley. It is expected that the commissioning of flights would attract more foreign tourists to the former summer capital of the country.

The natural scenic beauty of Simla and its past would continue to attract tourists in the future though it has outlived the purpose for which it was developed.

Bibliography

Census

Anonymous: Report on the Simla Census of July 26, 1904.

Kaul, H.K.: Report on the Summer Census of Simla, 1911, Lahore, 1912.

Census of India 1951: Punjab District Census Handbook, Vol. 6, Simla District, Simla, 1952.

Census of India 1961: Punjab District Census Handbook No. 6, Simla District, Chandigarh, 1965.

Census 1971, Series 7, Himachal Pradesh, District Census Handbook, Simla District, Simla, 1977, 2 vols.

Gazetteers

Hunter, W.W.: Imperial Gazetteer of India, London, 1881, Vol. VIII, Simla, 345-51.

——: Imperial Gazetteer of India, London, 1887, Vol. XII, Simla, 420-501.

India Government: Imperial Gazetteer of India, Oxford, 1908, Vol. XXII, Simla, 376-88.

Punjab Government: Gazetteer of Simla District, 1888-89, Calcutta, 1889.

——: Punjab District Gazetteer, Vol. VIIIA, Simla District, 1904, Lahore, 1908.

Guides

Anonymous: Thackers' Guide to Simla based on Travellers' Guide to Simla, Calcutta, 1902.

Carey, W.H.: Guide to Simla, Calcutta, 1870.

Harrop, F. Beresford: Thackers' New Guide to Simla, Calcutta, 1925.

Dept. of Tourism: Simla, Delhi, 1955.

Jubbal, Bh. and Rekha: New Tourist Guide to Simla and Adjoining Country, Simla, 1972.

Towelle, W. Morch: Handbook and Guide to Simla with sketch map, Simla, 1876.

Reports

Dawar, L.R.: Economic Survey of Simla Rickshawmen, Lahore, 1934.

A.P. Ecostat: A Brochure on Simla City, Simla, 1973.

Punjab Ecostat: Statistical Abstracts of Simla District, Chandigarh, 1963.

Punjab Govt.: Punjab Government Records, Lahore, 1911.

——: Report on Simla Extension Committee, 1898, Simla, 1898.

——: Report of the Simla Improvement Committee, Simla, 1907.

——: Report of the Simla Improvement Committee, Simla, 1914.

——: Report of the Simla House Accommodation Committee, Simla, 1917.

——: Report of the Simla Water Works Committee, Simla, 1904.

——: Report of the Simla Sanitary Investigation Committee, Simla, 1905.

Simla Municipal Committee: Annual Administration Report of Municipal Committee, Simla (Annual).

——: Simla Municipality Bye-laws, Simla, 1937.

Settlement Reports

Anderson, J.D.: Final Settlement of the Simla District, 1915-16, Lahore, 1917.

Wace, E.C.: Final Report on the First Regular Settlement of the Simla District in the Punjab, 1881-83, Calcutta, 1884.

Books on Simla

Anand, J.K.: Simla's First-Century and Who's Who, Simla, 1938.

Anonymous: Simla Directory, Simla, 1882, 1894, 1895.

Barr, Pat and Desmond Ray: Simla: A Hill Station in British India, London, 1978.

Bastavala, D.: Simla, Bombay, 1925.

Buck, Edward J.: Simla Past and Present, Calcutta, 1904, 1925.

Denyer, P.H.: Simla Amateur Dramatic Club, 1837-1937, Simla, 1937.

Dracott, Alic Elizabeth: Simla Village Tales, London, 1906.

French, Charles J.: A Concise and Cursory Narrative of Simla in the Himalaya Mountain, Agra, 1853.

Garbett, Colin: One Hundred Years of Christ Church, Simla, 1844-1944, Lahore, 1944.

Jailal: Speech delivered by Sir Jai Lal, President, House-owners and Merchants Association of Simla, Annual meeting held on 24th August, 1940.

Kanwar, Pamela: Urban History of Simla, H.P. University, Ph.D. Dissertation, 1983.

Thomas George Powell: Views of Simla, London, 1846.

Wilkinson, J.E.: Parochial History of Simla, 1836-1903, Simla, 1903.

General Books

Allan, Charles: Plain Tales from the Raj, London, 1975.

Allan, Charles: Raj: A Scrap Book of India, London, 1977.

Archer, Edward C.: Tours in Upper India and in parts of the Himalayan Mountains, London, 1833, 2 vols.

Barr, Pat: The Memsahib, London, 1976.

Bence-Jones, Mark: The Viceroys of India, London.

Bhattacharjee, Arun: History of Modern India, 1757-1947, Delhi.

Birkenhead (Lord): Rudyard Kipling, London, 1978.

Bradley, John: Lady Curzon's India, London.

Brecher, Michael: Nehru: A Political Biography, London, 1959.

Caine, W.S.: Picturesque India: London, 1898.

Campbell-Johnson: Mission with Mountbatten, London, 1953.

Carrington, Charles: Rudyard Kipling: His Life and Works. London, 1955.

Collin, L. and Lapierre, D: Freedom at Midnight, Delhi, 1976.

Cumming, C.F.G.: In the Himalayas and on the Indian Plains, London, 1866.

Curzon of Kedleston: British Government in India, London, 1925, 2 vols.

Curzon, Marques: Viceroy's India, London, 1984.

Das, M.N.: India Under Morley and Minto, London, 1964.

Dennis, Kincaid: British Social Life in India, 1608-1937, London, 1973.

Dufferin, Marques Ava: Our Viceregal Life in India, London, 1889, 2 vols.

Dunbar George: History of India, London, 1949, 2 vols.

Durga Dass: India: Curzon to Nehru and After, Delhi, 1969.

Eden, Emily: Up the Country: Letter written to Sister from the Upper Provinces of India, London, 1866, 2 vols.

Edward, Michael: Bound in Exile, London, 1969.

Edward, Michael: British India 1772-1947, London, 1967.

Farrell, J.G.: The Hill Station, Delhi, 1981.

Fitze, Kanneth: Twilight of the Maharajas, London, 1956.

Fitzroy, Yvoune: Courts and Camps in India, Impressions of Viceregal Tour, 1921-24, London, 1926.

Francis, Charles Edward: Sketches of Native Life in India with Views of Rajpootana, Simlah etc., London, 1848.

French, Charles J: Journal of a Tour in Upper Hindustan performed during the years 1838-1839 with Camp of the Right Hon'ble, The Earl of Auckland, Governor-General of India, Agra, 1854.

Ghosh, Sudhir: Gandhi's Emissary, London, 1967.

Gould, B.J.: Jewel in the Crown, London, 1957.

Hedin, Sven: Trans-Himalaya, London, 1908, 2 vols.

Hirschmann, Edwin: White Mutiny, Delhi, 1980.

Jacquemont, Victor: Letter from India, London, 1834, 2 vols.

Kincaid, Dennis: British Social Life in India, 1608-1937, London, 1973.

Kipling, Rudyard: Plain Tales from the Hills, London, 1964.

Lloyd, Wm. and Gerard Alexander: Narrative of a Journey from Caunpor to the Boorendo Pass in the Himalaya Mountains, London, 1840, 2 vols.

Mahajan, Mehar Chand: Looking Back, Delhi, 1963.

Majumdar, A.K.: Advent of Independence, Bombay, 1963.

Malhotra, P.L.: Administration of Lord Elgin in India, Delhi, 1979.

Masani, R.P.: British In India, OUP, 1960.

Mason, Philip: Shaft in the Sun, London, 1978.

Mehrotra, S.R.: Towards India's Freedom and Partition, Delhi, 1979.

Menon, V.P.: Transfer of Power in India, Delhi, 1957.

Mersey, V: Viceroys and Governors-General of India, London, 1949.

Misra, J.P.: Administration of India under Lord Lansdowne, Delhi, 1975.

Moon, E. Penderel: Divide and Quit, London, 1961.

Moorhouse, Geoffery: India Britannica, London, 1983.

Morris, Deborah: With Scarlet Majors, London, 1960.

Morris, James: Pax Britannica, London, 1979.

Morris, Jones: Stones of the Empire, London, 1983.

Mosley, Leonard: Last Days of British Raj, London, 1961.

Moulton, E.C.: Lord Northbrook's Indian Administration, 1872-76, London, 1968.

Muggeridge, Malcolm: Chronicles of Wasted Time, London, 1972, 2 vols.

Mundy, G.C.: Pen and Pencil Sketches, being the journal of a tour in India, London, 1832, 2 vols.

Nayak, R.K.: Vithalbhai Patel: Patriot and President, Delhi, 1976.

Norman, Dorothy: Nehru: The First Sixty Years, Bombay, 1965, Vol 2.

Pakistan Historical Society, Karachi: History of the Freedom Movement, Delhi, 1984, Vol 3.

Philip, C.H. ed: The Partition of India: Politics and Perspectives, 1935-1947, London, 1970.

Prinsep, Vol C.: Glimpses of Imperial India, London, 1878.

Punjab Govt.: Punjab Government Records, Lahore, 1911, 8 vols.

Rai Mangat: Commitment My Style, Delhi, 1973.

Randhawa, M.S.: Travels in the Western Himalayas, Delhi, 1974.

Richardson, H.E.: Tibet and its History, London, 1962.

Russell, W.H.: My Diary in India in the year 1958-59, London, 1860.

Sharp, Henry: Good-bye India, London, 1946.

Stanford, J.K.: Ladies in the Sun, London, 1962.

Sykes, Percy: History of Afghanistan, Delhi, 1981, Vol 2.

Taylor, William: Thirty-eight Years in India from Jaganath to the Himalaya Mountains, London, 1881, 2 vols.

Thomson, Thomas: Western Himalaya and Tibet, London, 1852.

Tinker, Hugh: Experiment with Freedom: India and Pakistan, Delhi, 1979.

Tinker, Hugh: The Ordeal of Love: C.F. Andrews and India, Delhi, 1979.

Van Der Sleen, W.G.N.: Four Months Camping in the Himalaya, London, 1929.

Waley, S.D.: Montagou: Memoirs and Account of his Visit to India, London, 1964.

Wavell, Archibald: The Viceroy's Journal ed. by P. Moon, London, 1973.

Wedderburn, Wm.: Allan Octavian Hume, Delhi, 1838.

White, G.F.: Views in India, chiefly among the Himalaya Mountains, London, 1838.

Wilson, Andrew: Abode of Snow, London, 1875.

Wilson (Lady): Letters from India, London, 1911.

Wolpert, Stanley: Jinnah of Pakistan, N.Y., 1984.

Woodford, Paggy: Rise of the Raj, London, 1978.

Woodruff, Philip: The Men who Ruled India: The Guardian, London, 1954.

Wyman, F. F.: From Calcutta to the Snowy Ranges, being the narrative of a trip through the Upper Provinces of India to the Himalayas, London, 1866.

Zaidi, A. Moin: Way out to Freedom, Delhi, 1973.

STATISTICAL INFORMATION ON SIMLA

Location: 118 kilometers North-East of Chandigarh. Capital of Himachal Pradesh. Latitude 31° 06′ N and Longitude 77° 31′ E.

Elevation: 2,150 meters (average) above Mean Sea Level.

Area: 5,131 square kilometers of the Simla district, and about 18 square kilometers of Simla town.

Climate: Very cold from December to February with occasional snow-fall; cold from March to May and September to November getting warm in the afternoons but remaining cold during nights; Rainy during June to August when monsoon breaks over the region.

Temperature: Winters—Max 18.33°C, Min — 5.55°C
Summers—Max 32.77°C, Min — 1.11°C.

Rainfall: 70″ (average).

Population: 70,604 (1981 Census) nearly 1 lakh now.

Languages spoken: Hindi, Pahari, English, Punjabi.

Bus links: Delux/ordinary buses every hour from Delhi and almost every half hour from Chandigarh. Buses available for all towns in Himachal Pradesh.

Rail link: Narrow-guage railway line from Kalka at the foot-hills of Shiwalik ranges. Three daily train services and a rail car service between Kalka and Simla every day. Kalka itself is well-connected on broadguage with Delhi and Chandigarh.

Taxi Service: Full or share taxies available from Kalka.

Air link: Daily flight service from Delhi via Chandigarh.

Distance (from): Delhi . . . . 370 kilometers
Kalka . . . . 88 kilometers
Chandigarh . . . . 118 kilometers
Dehradun . . . . 245 kilometers
Kasauli . . . . 78 kilometers
Bilaspur . . . . 91 kilometers
Narkanda . . . . 64 kilometers
Rampur . . . . 130 kilometers
Paonta Sahib . . . . . . 184 kilometers
Nahan . . . . 145 kilometers
Chail . . . . 45 kilometers
Kalpa . . . . 245 kilometers

Index